D0760265

# GUY LALIBERTÉ

## THE FABULOUS LIFE OF
## THE CREATOR OF CIRQUE DU SOLEIL

# Guy Laliberté

## The Fabulous Life of
## the Creator of Cirque du Soleil

A Biography

by

# Ian Halperin

Transit

Thompson-Nicola Regional District
Library System
300-465 VICTORIA STREET
KAMLOOPS, BC    V2C 2A9

Published by Transit Publishing Inc.
© 2009 Transit Publishing Inc. and Ian Halperin
The reproduction or transmission of any part of this publication in any form or
by any means, electronic, mechanical, recording, or otherwise, or storage in a
retrieval system, without the prior consent of the publisher, is an infringement
of copyright law. In the case of photocopying or other reprographic
production of the material, a licence must be obtained from the Canadian
Copyright Licensing Agency (Access Copyright) before proceeding.

ISBN: 978-1-926745-15-2 (U.S.)
ISBN: 978-1-926745-14-5 (Canada)

Editing: Suzan Ayscough, Shannon Partridge
Proofreading: Timothy Niedermann
Cover design: François Turgeon
Text design and composition: Jonathan Stone, Nassim Bahloul
Illumination: Gratia Ionescu

Cover picture: Keystone Press Agency Ldt.
Kike Calvo/KPA-ZUMA/KEYSTONE Press.
© Michel Ponomareff / Ponopresse / International / Gamma / Eyedea Presse


Back cover picture: François Turgeon


Transit Publishing Inc.
1996 St-Joseph Boulevard East
Montreal, Quebec
CANADA
H2H 1E3
Telephone 1-514-273-0123

Printed and Bound in Canada

101868068X

# Books by the Same Author

Who Killed Kurt Cobain?

Love & Death: The Murder of Kurt Cobain

Fire and Rain: The James Taylor Story

Shut up and Smile: Supermodels, the Dark Side

Bad and Beautiful:

Inside the Dazzling and Deadly World of Supermodels

Best CEOs, How the Wild, Wild Web Was Won

Céline Dion: Behind the Fairytale

Miss Supermodel America

Unmasked: The Final Years of Michael Jackson


# Coming Soon
# From Transit Publishing

Brangelina: Angelina Jolie & Brad Pitt

Scientology: The Religion of the Stars?

# TABLE OF CONTENTS

# FOREWORD

The first time I met Guy Laliberté, I was struck by how much we had in common. We both started out as street performers—buskers—perfecting our craft and learning how to interact with people as if our very livelihoods depended on it. They often did. We both have used the understanding of human nature that we cultivated on the streets to excel in our chosen fields, although Guy has a few more zeros in his bank balance to attest to his success than I. We both also have an unquenchable thirst for life's pleasures, balanced with a passion for social justice—traits that we know are not incompatible.

Our paths crossed again indirectly during a crisis he was experiencing in his personal life, and I found myself very conflicted. Guy Laliberté, I sensed, was a man of destiny. Who was I to interfere with that destiny? Yet I had some place in all this. For a period of time I had been in a close platonic friendship with the woman with whom he was at war. The question forced me to examine my core values and the nature of loyalty, and, ultimately, to make some hard choices.

I knew that Guy and I shared another thing in common. Our children had played together for years, and we had both strongly instilled in our kids a sense of right and wrong. What would it say to my daughter if I didn't stand up for what I knew was right? Almost all the terrible things in our society can be traced to a quest for money. I felt that it was about time somebody said "Stop!" about this particular money grab.

Although I regret the inevitable damage it caused to my friendship with his ex, I don't regret my decision to side with Guy. He is a man who, throughout the tortuous years of his painful conflicts, has behaved with quiet dignity, remarkable restraint, and a strength of character that has made him one of the most fascinating, successful, and enigmatic characters in Quebec and Canadian society.

When I set out to tell his story and make sense of how we both reached this crossroads, I also discovered just how much people still don't know about the rise of Guy Laliberté and Cirque du Soleil.

*Ian Halperin, May 2009*

# DEDICATION

To anyone who has ever performed on the street and thought it wasn't possible to go further in life.

# Acknowledgements

First and foremost, thanks to legendary Quebec publisher and author Pierre Turgeon for believing in this book. I have known Pierre for more than a decade and have always found him to be a great visionary, a consummate pro, and a first class human being. This book could not have been undertaken without his vision.

I'd also like to thank the remarkable team at Transit Publishing, including Pierre's incredibly gifted son François and this book's editor, Suzan Ayscough, who was wonderful to work with. Suzan also contributed the Life is a Vicious Circus kicker.

This book was greatly facilitated by sources who revealed information to me that they had never before discussed with anyone. I am grateful for their trust. Thanks to those who spoke on the record without fear of repercussions. I have changed the names of many people in the book who still have close ties to Cirque du Soleil and Guy Laliberté and who were not willing to take the same risk.

*Pure entertainment is not an egotistical lady singing boring songs onstage for two hours and people in tuxes clapping whether they like it or not. It's the real performers on the street who can hold people's attention and keep them from walking away.*

—Andy Kaufman

# PROLOGUE

March 2008. Almost 3 AM. Manhattan is buzzing, even this late at night—or early in the morning. I have just filmed an interview with *New York Times* number-one best-selling author, Andrew Morton, for whom I arranged a live appearance on Joey Reynolds's syndicated radio show.

Morton, you may recall, is the author to whom Princess Diana confided her most intimate secrets. He is also the writer hired to pen Monica Lewinsky's memoirs after her historic tryst with President Clinton. His latest tome, a biography of actor and devout Scientologist Tom Cruise, hit number one in its first week of sales. Morton is in a jovial mood. I've tagged along to film him for a multimedia website we are both trying to get off the ground.

I first met Morton when he showed up unexpectedly at my film premiere at New York's National Arts Clubs a couple of weeks earlier.

I was most flattered when he called my film about going undercover as a gay actor in Hollywood "Borat, but with substance." A couple of days later I contacted him and described my website idea. He loved it, and each day since, we've met at his midtown hotel suite to work on a pitch to potential investors.

During the cab ride back from downtown, where Reynolds's show is taped, Morton tells my assistant Alison and me that he is trying to come up with a subject for his next book.

"Maybe Angelina and Brad, but I don't think I'll do Spitzer."

Spitzer is the New York governor forced to resign last year because of his dalliances with hookers.

"I definitely need someone who is big and who has not been done before. Anyone have any ideas?"

Bingo! Immediately a thought comes to my head. I know of one person who has become the richest and most powerful person in showbiz, and I am certain a biography about him has never been done before. I think hard about it for a couple of minutes before blurting out his name. "I know the person who could sell you a million copies, if it's done right," I tell Morton.

"Has there ever been a book published about him?"

"Definitely not."

After Morton begs me two more times to tell him, I say it: " Guy Laliberté."

"I've never heard of him. Who the hell is he?"

I tell him again. By the end of the cab ride, I have briefed Morton about Laliberté and his incredible life. Morton is fascinated. He is interested in writing the book. But when I arrive back at my apartment I get a call from Morton asking why I am not writing the book about Laliberté myself, if I believe it could sell so many copies.

I have never considered it before tonight. By the end of

the phone call, Morton has promised me he'll back off writing about Guy if I want to do it myself. "It's your idea, and I think it's more suited to you because you know all the key players," he says.

Needless to say, I take his advice.

* * *

February 2002. Another wintry night. The blowing snow whips, bites, and stuns without an ounce of mercy. It's all part of Montreal's charm. It's not so charming, however, to be blowing a running nose all the time. As a snow lover, I am nevertheless delighted to be going out on another night like this.

There is a silver Mercedes waiting for me in front of my apartment in Montreal's west-end middle-class district, Notre Dame de Grace. The driver is a tall, stunning Brazilian woman wearing sunglasses. She is exceedingly polite and takes me for a drive downtown. I love the architecture of Montreal, combined with the steep hills and intimate atmosphere. I feel grand.

The woman splutters in broken English about how she misses the beautiful beaches of her native Brazil, especially at this time of the year. She lashes out against Quebec culture; she calls it "North Pole politics." She criticizes the province's English people, then gives equal time to knocking the province's French. It doesn't seem as if she is thrilled to be in her adopted country, Canada.

She makes a quick call on her cell. When her number gets through, she barks at someone in Portuguese. It sounds as if she is about to hit the person through the receiver. "It's my Latin temperament," she says. "Usually, I'm a very calm person." I just sit there, dazed and numb, writing in my head my own exit strategy from this whacko. We only met yesterday afternoon. She is Rizia Moreira, mother to three of the children of Guy Laliberté, the billionaire owner of Cirque du Soleil.

As she drives further, I ask her to slow down. She is not driving safely on the hazardous, icy roads. She seems intent on asserting her ego. Her driving frightens the life out of me, as she speeds like a hot dog sledding down a hill. She slams on the brakes and skids her brand new Mercedes sports wagon through four inches of fresh snow on top of black ice. I think, "Why spoil a delightful winter night's drive by having to file an insurance claim?"

Finally, we reach our destination. Moreira pulls up in front of Thailand Restaurant in the trendy Mile End district. Throughout the fancy dinner, she makes me feel wildly popular as she strokes my ego. She tells me it has been a long time since she has met someone as interesting and dynamic. I am flattered.

Hindsight will later show me that this evening I am also most naïve. Little do I suspect that this tall supermodel type has only one thing in mind—to exploit a family connection to help with her issues with Laliberté.

For hours, she regales me with stories about her past. She confides that she can't wait to travel the world after her issues with her ex-lover are resolved.

"Montreal is not the best place to meet people," she tells me. "I'm so glad we have met. I have been so lonely ever since I split with Guy. All our friends took his side. It has made my life lonely and miserable."

Even though I think she's nuts, I like Moreira in these early days. She is funny, wild, and mischievous; she is also horribly insecure. Insecurity makes everyone self-destructive, but as I will later learn, Moreira takes it to a whole new level.

I learn about the excesses of her fast-paced life. She has an unparalleled taste for luxury. She loves pomp and show. Everything she wears is custom tailored for her by the world's leading fashion designers. She enjoys every perquisite that life affords only the richest and most famous, including household staff, trips to different parts of the world every few weeks, and every pair of Manolo Blahnik shoes you can cram into a closet. She spends money like there is no tomorrow.

At first I can't figure out how she affords it all. She tries to give me the impression she is from a wealthy family, which I will later learn is the furthest thing from the truth. I will learn instead that her current lifestyle is only possible thanks to the generosity of Guy Laliberté.

When the waiter offers us the dessert menu, we bow over with laughter as we hear his question: "How long have you two been married?" Moreira laughs so hard she falls off her chair, and every person in the restaurant stares at us. They can't take their eyes off us the rest of the night; perhaps they can't decide if we are crazy or not.

As the night progresses, I try talking to her about life in Brazil and how she came to Canada. But at this memorable first dinner, all she wants to talk about is how angry she is at her ex-lover of ten years. Clearly, she is obsessed with the man who has dumped her and who is trying to begin a new life, however unsuccessfully.

She is intense. She loves Laliberté so much it is killing her, she says. Laliberté never loved her back hard enough. He was never committed enough. He wasn't a dedicated enough father to their three children.

My B.S. detector goes off. I've learned my own life lessons, and I know this woman's story is only one side of the equation. I know that Laliberté will have his own version which will differ immensely. Eventually I will understand why he fled from her as if running away to join the circus, even though he already owned Cirque du Soleil—he was trying to escape what he called "Rizia's Circus."

I understand one thing clearly from the get-go: Moreira and Laliberté had a most volatile relationship, and he had told her over and over again that he couldn't take it anymore. I will later learn from close friends of the couple that she ignored his cries for change until the day he walked out. I learn from her that she was intent on staying together forever, no matter how ugly things got, including drug abuse, infidelity, and excessive shouting and domestic disputes.

"Guy thinks he's larger than life," she tells me. "He would be out all night partying with young girls while I stayed home watching the kids. He had so many women behind my back. He tried to hide it, but I caught him each time. Several times, he transmitted to me sexual diseases he picked up from other people. I confronted him, and he didn't know what to say.

"He made my life miserable. I tried over and over to work it out with Guy, but it was like talking to a brick wall. I should have listened to my family and not hooked up with him in the first place. I was too young, too infatuated with him. He was able to manipulate me any way he wanted."

As we dip into the mouth-watering dessert of fried bananas topped with vanilla ice cream, it is apparent how lost she is. She seems to hate herself. She says she likes alcohol because it makes her hate herself less. She hates men—loathes them—even though she keeps a string of boyfriends in cities all over the world. She tells me that men have been trying to screw her since she was seven years old. Family members, she says, tried to screw her. Her neighbors tried. Every man who walked into her family's modest home in Brazil tried. "I love sex, but I hate men," she tells me. "Most men I've dated are sharks. I can't seem to meet the right guy."

Back at her apartment, I gush over the spectacular views of the city. From the corner windows I can see the top of Mont Royal, the mountain that sits in middle of Montreal. The pad is expansive, with a large living space that forms her main entertaining area. It is filled with expensive and exclusive pieces of furniture designed by top interior designers. An exotic living room set-up and imported oak dining room set catch my eye.

She makes me a cup of herbal tea and tells me her ex has the kids for the week; that's why we are all alone. Whenever Laliberté takes the kids, she explains, he also takes the hired help—two nannies and a cook.

Suddenly, she begins to cry. She tells me how disappointed she is with the recent turn of events in her life and how much she misses her old life with Laliberté. "Now, everything is gone. Guy has taken everything away from me," she complains.

As I look around at her lavish surroundings, her sorrow is lost on me. I am not about to throw a pity party for her. Is it my job to comfort her? What I really feel like telling her is that she's spoiled, and why does she complain so much. Only a hundred or so women in the entire world must live in luxury the way she does. She just sits here and feels sorry for herself.

Her cell phone rings. It is Laliberté, her bald-headed ex-lover with a strong street accent in both French and English. Within ten seconds she starts screaming at him for calling her so late. He wants to update her on their youngest child, who is fighting a cold. She yells at him in Portuguese for almost two minutes before banging down the phone. He immediately calls back. Clearly, she has said something to him that disquiets him. Perhaps she has something on him, some evidence, something concrete that could damage his reputation and career. At one point during the conversation, she threatens to go to the police. I really can't figure it all out. After banging the phone down again, she storms into the bathroom in disgust. I cool my heels by watching TV for half an hour before she re-emerges.

Then something happens that night that I will never be able to understand. It is almost 3 AM. She asks me to lie down on the cold floor. She unbuttons my shirt and takes off my pants, then my socks. I am as naked as a jaybird. She looks me up and down with interest, and visions of having sex with her enter my mind. I can't help but think how many men would kill to be in my position right now.

It wouldn't be my first intimate encounter with the rich and famous. Earlier this year, I finished my book about going undercover as a male model; during my research I slept with several well known supermodels and actresses. But sleeping with the ex-lover of one of the world's wealthiest and most known billionaires would certainly not damage my ego.

Suddenly, she hops on my back, barefooted. She is on me, standing upright, and starts applying hard foot strokes to my back. She tells me she wants to open up all my chakras and release my inner toxins and melt away all my pain and stress. I think she is completely out of her mind. But as she continues, my body starts to feel relaxed. I am amazed by what her tootsies are capable of, especially when she digs into the sore spots under my lower spine. She is as quiet and agile as a mouse. Fittingly, the ex-lover of the circus leader executes her footwork as if she were an accomplished tightrope walker. She explains that she picked up this foot compression technique while staying at the world's most expensive hotel, in Dubai.

"It was a seven-star hotel at $30,000 a night," she says. "They had the world's top massage therapists there. That's how I learned to do all this."

Within an hour I fall asleep, right on her living room floor. The next morning I wake up around 7 AM. She is sound asleep in the next room. My first twenty-four hours with this Amazon-type woman have made for one of my most memorable nights ever. No wonder she dated the man who owned the circus; she lives her life as if she were the featured act. Soon, she will get her wish.

# Part I

1

The circus is the only ageless delight that you can buy for money," Ernest Hemingway once wrote. There is, of course, one other great and timeless pleasure—for adults. It is thus probably more accurate to say that the circus is the only entertainment that has consistently delighted young and old alike.

The modern circus, the forebearer of Cirque du Soleil, can be traced back to the middle of the eighteenth century. Its original ancestor dates from millennia before that, in ancient Rome and beyond. The Roman circus featured chariot races, equestrian shows, staged battles, trained animal exhibitions, jugglers, and acrobats. The Latin name for that building comes from an even earlier time, when the Greeks staged chariot races and animal exhibitions in the *kirkos*—the circle or ring.

In Rome, the circus consisted of tiers of seats running parallel with the sides of the course, forming a crescent around one of the ends. The lower seats were reserved for persons or rank and VIPs; there were also various state boxes for the person hosting the event and his friends.

Significantly, in ancient Rome, the circus was the only public spectacle where men and women were not separated.

Cleo Paskal, in her chronicle of the tradition of circus for the online newspaper *The Independent*, writes that the most famous circus in the Roman Empire was the Circus Maximus in Rome. Built more than two thousand five hundred years ago and rebuilt by Julius Caesar, it was said to seat more than three hundred thousand spectators, who paid to see chariot races, athletic competitions, and gladiatorial fighting.

It wasn't all fun and games, Paskal adds. "Interspersed with the animal acts were bloody, brutal contests, often cheered on by rioting chariot hooligans. High on the bill at one of the arenas, the Circus Neronis, was the creation of Christian martyrs."

Not until the fall of the Roman Empire did circuses become more family friendly, when small bands of travelling entertainers—acrobats, jugglers, and troubadours—roamed the countryside performing in small towns. The wandering minstrels of the Middle Ages were a by-product of these bands. Occasionally, the troupes featured a performing bear, a contortionist, or a tumbling acrobat.

The first modern European circus is said to have been staged on the banks of London's Thames River by Philip Astley, in the mid-eighteenth century. A former army sergeant-major, Astley awed crowds with his trick riding. He performed seemingly impossible acrobatic maneuvers upon his horse as he rode it around an enclosed circular space. While there is some debate over whether Astley ever described his show as such, the *Oxford English Dictionary* lists the 1791 book The *History of the Royal Circus*, about Philip Astley's troupe, as the first written use of the word to describe the modern circus.

After two years, the crowds were getting bored by the same old horse act, so Astley added jugglers, clowns, and tumblers to the spectacle. The success of his show spawned a series of imitators, who gradually added wild animal acts, such as tamed lions, to their own equestrian shows. Before long, Astley was performing for the crowned heads of Europe, including a much celebrated performance for Louis XV at Versailles. Following this, the continent saw the creation of numerous circus troupes.

It wasn't until 1793, less than two decades after the birth of the U.S., that the first circus came to North America. John Bill Ricketts, a student of Astley's main competitor, took his show to Philadelphia, where President George Washington and his wife Martha were among its biggest fans. The performance mostly consisted of equestrian acts, with a few tumblers thrown in for good measure. In 1797, Ricketts set up a circus amphitheatre in New York; the same year he visited Montreal for six months to establish what is thought to be Canada's first circus. It wouldn't be the last.

* * *

When Guy Laliberté was a boy, his parents took him to see the Ringling Bros. and Barnum & Bailey Circus. He would later say he didn't find it funny, although perhaps this is a myth he later created to put down the only circus in the world more famous than his own. It did, nevertheless, inspire him to read a biography of P.T. Barnum, the greatest circus showman the world has ever known. The Ringling Bros. and Barnum & Bailey Circus website reports that Phineas Taylor Barnum never claimed the line "There's a sucker born every minute," although we might suppose he embraced the concept. In fact, the phrase was coined by one of his competitors.

Born in 1810 in Connecticut, Barnum aspired early to the showmanship of selling curiosities. At just twenty-five years old, he hired Joice Heth, whom he exhibited on tour as the world's oldest woman, and who earned him back his investment many times over.

A few years later, Barnum had moved up in scale and was exhibiting "500,000 natural and artificial curiosities from every corner of the globe" in his New York City museum. Never one to be outwitted by a dollar, Barnum had a sign posted in the museum that told people, "This Way to the Egress"—*egress* is another word for exit. Barnum's patrons, eager to see a real live egress, would have to pay another quarter to re-enter the museum.

At one point in the 1870s, after Barnum had expanded into the circus business, his show covered five acres and welcomed ten thousand patrons at a time. His circuses were grossing hundreds of thousands of dollars per year, even in the age of the five-cent loaf of bread. He had long since written and published his 1854 autobiography, *The Life of P.T. Barnum, Written by Himself.* After many years of dabbling in several partnerships and forms of circus, Barnum and James Anthony Bailey solidified a business relationship and in 1888 launched the first American tour of the Barnum & Bailey Greatest Show On Earth.

The Ringling Bros. and Barnum & Bailey website tells us that Barnum's last words before his death in April 1891 were supposedly about the cash-box take on the circus's latest show at New York's Madison Square Garden. "Ask Bailey what the box office was at the Garden last night," he is reported to have said.

The website cites *Life* magazine's epithet for Barnum: "The patron saint of promoters." Although Guy Laliberté's success is rooted in a very different philosophy from that of the master showman to whom he's often compared, some might say he has a better claim to the title than P.T. Barnum.

* * *

When the seeds of Cirque du Soleil were being planted in the early 1980s, Quebec had only a small circus tradition to speak of. Quebecers were familiar with the traditional circus arts, as the grand American circuses such as Ringling Bros. often toured through Montreal or Quebec City. And a fledgling native circus had seen light, thanks to "the world's strongest man."

Louis Cyr, one of Quebec's best-known showmen of the nineteenth century, was born in Napierville in 1863. When he was very young, Cyr's mother decided that he should let his hair grow like Samson in the Bible; his hair would become one of his many distinctive trademarks. When Cyr was only eighteen, he travelled to Boston and entered his first strongman contest, in which he hefted a full-grown horse off the ground. His most famous feat also took place in Boston, where he lifted upon his back a platform holding eighteen men. In Quebec, he once pushed a rail freight car up an incline. These exploits were widely celebrated in his hometown province, where Cyr became the stuff of legend.

Cyr decided to capitalize on his growing fame and formed the Troupe Cyr. He left his work as a Montreal policeman and toured Quebec to show off his feats of strength. He was recruited as a star attraction for the John Robinson Circus, with whom he toured extensively and performed his act of holding above his head a platform upon which two bicyclists circled. The act attracted the attention of the Ringling brothers, who incorporated the circus and Cyr into their own big top. At the end of the nineteenth century, the strongman returned to Quebec to form the Cyr Circus and toured French-speaking Canada with a variety of performers. His act never used animals.

When Cirque du Soleil came along nearly one hundred years later,

Cyr may have been an inspiration, although he by no means embodied the tradition that Cirque's founders drew upon. Nor did they draw from the grand spectacles of Barnum and Bailey. Instead, it can be said that the seed of Cirque du Soleil was germinated in the fields of rural Vermont and on the streets of Quebec City.

2 While it may be true that Guy Laliberté is the founder of Cirque du Soleil, most people agree that it was Gilles Ste-Croix who planted the seeds for it and without whom there would be no Cirque. Ste-Croix has said that if Laliberté is the father of the Cirque, "then I'm the grandfather." But he also adds something that may be a more accurate reflection of the history: "I founded Guy Laliberté."

Ste-Croix says he became a street performer by accident. "I was going to be an architect," he recalls. "But I just couldn't keep up with the workload, so I quit." He says he had always wanted to be in show business, but his traditionalist parents frowned on such a life and pushed him to work towards a "real" job.

Drawn to the counterculture that had swept Canada while he was groing up, and which had bypassed his tiny, rural-Quebec town, Ste-Croix wanted to wander. He packed up and travelled to British Columbia, where he learned English. In fact, his English is much better than that of most of his colleagues and is a skill that would prove important in paving the way for Cirque's eventual success in the United States.

Out in western Canada, Ste-Croix picked magic mushrooms, smoked a lot of pot, and immersed himself in the back-to-the-earth movement, which still thrived on the west coast, long after having faded in the rest of the country.

As the '60s ended and the counterculture of that decade gave way to the materialism of the '70s, many BC hippies formed socialist-style communes, similar to Israeli kibbutzim, where the work and the fruits of the labour were shared. They were also influenced by similar movements down the coast in California, especially the Haight-Ashbury-inspired hippie movement in San Francisco. Indeed, many of the residents of the B.C. communes were Americans who had fled to Canada during the Vietnam war to avoid the draft. But politics often took a back seat to pleasure. Mostly participants played music, smoked pot, and had a lot of sex. Free love reigned.

"I lived with these freaks trying to make a change in society," Ste-Croix later told Tony Babinski in the Cirque's official history, *20 Years Under the Sun.*

Eventually Ste-Croix returned to Quebec, partly from homesickness, because his parents were pushing him to return to reality. All through his subsequent, short-lived architecture career, he knew that it wasn't for him. He had discovered in Quebec a number of communes and cooperatives that had sprung up and was itching to return to the nomadic life. Unlike those he had experienced on the west coast years before, these communes were strongly rooted in socialism and artistic endeavours and were attracting artists, musicians, street performers, and craftspeople. The drugs and sex were just as prominent as they had been in B.C., but now there was also the headiness of nationalism added to the mix.

At one such commune, which he recalls as being very socialist in its philosophy, he remembers, "You couldn't bring a guitar in unless it was for everyone." The communes were connected to a series of Montreal-based cooperatives selling everything from produce and crafts to poetry books and musical instruments.

The turning point for Ste-Croix and the future Cirque du Soleil came while he was living at a commune in Victoriaville. There was an apple orchard where each member was expected to participate in the harvest. One day, as Ste-Croix was climbing a ladder to reach the highest branches, he thought to himself that his task would be easier if the ladder were attached to his legs. He decided to make himself a pair of stilts. An American working at the commune saw him cavorting around on them and mentioned a theatre company in Vermont where they performed on stilts. Ste-Croix was intrigued.

The Bread and Puppet Theater company was actually formed in New York City's Lower East Side in the early '60s. A German expatriate named Peter Schumann had decided to combine puppet making and political theatre at rent strikes, community organizing events, and civil rights rallies. The name derives from the company's practice of distributing freshly baked bread to the audience as a means of creating community. Eventually, Schumann built a giant puppet theatre to put on shows protesting the Vietnam War. Photos from the most prominent anti-war rallies of the era feature the company's giant fifteen-foot puppets or Uncle Sams on stilts, towering over the crowds.

In 1970, Goddard College, which had a reputation for being radical, offered the company some land, which brought the Bread and Puppet Theater to Vermont. There, Schumann set up shop and began staging regular political pageants called the Domestic Resurrection Circus. By the time Gilles Ste-Croix decided to visit, the company had relocated not far from the Quebec border at a farm in Glover, Vermont, where they still reside today. When Ste-Croix visited the farm he struck up a friendship with Schumann, who asked him to take part in a Bread and Puppet pageant as a stilt-walker.

Ste-Croix only performed once with the company, but it had a profound effect on him. "This was what I wanted to do," he later recalled. "I thought, why can't we do this in Quebec?" Some believe the name of the Bread and Puppet pageants inspired Ste-Croix when his own band of intrepid Quebec artists decided to call their show a circus, despite the lack of animals and other acts traditionally associated with the name.

At the end of the '70s, a newly married Ste-Croix abandoned the idea of an office job for good. He moved to Baie-St-Paul, a thriving artist's colony up the St Lawrence river from Quebec City. Many people had drifted there from the communes in which he had lived on and off, over the years.

Seasonal accommodation was scarce in Baie-St-Paul because many of the residents, particularly the street performers, were transients who spent only summers there. By the time Ste-Croix arrived with his wife in the summer of 1979, a hostel called Le Balcon Vert was being established to provide lodging to newly arriving musicians and street performers. It would also be a place to congregate and perform. The idea appealed to Ste-Croix, and he accepted the job of managing the new venture. For him, it would be more than business; it would be an artistic adventure.

When a street performer named Guy Laliberté arrived at the hostel that summer looking for a place to stay for a few days, fate intervened in the life of Gilles Ste-Croix. He would hook up with the man whose path would be intertwined with his own for the next twenty years.

* * *

Guy Laliberté was born to a middle-class family in Quebec City in 1959, but his parents moved to Saint-Bruno, near Montreal, when he was a child. His father was a well-paid executive who worked for the giant aluminum company Alcan, and his mother was an aesthetician.

According to Chantal Leclerc, who has known him since childhood, "Guy was always a precocious child. By the age of two, he could already sing songs verbatim off the radio. He was also very mischievous. He'd disappear for hours on end, and his parents would have trouble finding him. He once rode his tricycle to the other part of town, and his parents had to look for him for hours. He was much smarter than your average kid. At age four he was already organizing lemonade sales outside his family's home."

In school, Laliberté did well without much effort, though he preferred music and sports to homework. He trained in martial arts from an early age and was an avid hockey fan, but his passion was art; he loved to sing and perform.

Leclerc recalls, "Whenever I went over to his family's home, there was always music, laughter, and warmth. He's been a romantic at heart, ever since anyone can remember. You could tell right away he was destined for a career in show business."

Laliberté trained in Quebec's rich folk-dancing tradition and also sang in several choirs. But another childhood friend, Serge Trudel, insists that, unlike many kids who get into showbiz because they're attention-starved, Laliberté was attracted to the performing arts for other reasons.

"He was a real poet, a real artist. I don't think he wanted attention, even though he liked being at the centre of things. He wanted to stretch the boundaries of art from an early age. He was a very curious kid."

By most accounts he was also a likeable kid. "No one was more popular than Guy. The Laliberté house was the place to be," remembers Trudel. "Everyone was welcome. It was always hopping there. Despite his popularity, Laliberté was no lady-killer. "He seemed shy around girls. He didn't really come into his own with girls until he hit his teens. And then we all know how he was later in life—a modern day Don Juan.

"Guy was the nicest boy, but only if you didn't cross him. He liked to be the leader, and if he didn't get his way, he would make sure he eventually got it. He could defend himself; if you picked on Guy you knew you'd be in for a battle. He did not go down easily. He wasn't tall, but he'd put up a fight and usually he'd win. He was a tough customer, but he was a tough guy with an artist's heart. From an early age he liked to live a poetic life."

Trudel adds, "Guy always said how important it was to be able to defend oneself spiritually and mentally, sort of the way he later did with Cirque du Soleil. It's amazing how advanced he was from a young age. His game plan was intact from the time he was a little boy. The exact same strategy paid off for him later in life."

Laliberté later described for Tony Babinksi how he first became attracted to show business as a sixteen-year-old high school student. It was during a concert by the renowned Cajun musician Zachary Richard at Montreal's Lafontaine Park.

"I had been interested in folk music since I was fourteen. I come from a musical family. My father played accordion, and we all sang. Zachary Richard was headlining the Quebec-Louisiana night. He was great, and during the show he extended an invitation to the audience. He said: 'You should come down to Louisiana and celebrate Mardi Gras with us.' The next day, I thought, 'Ok, I'll do it.'"

Displaying the entrepreneurial spirit that would later prove so valuable, Laliberté rallied his fellow students to raise money and organize a school trip to Louisiana. They held sales, concerts, and car washes and eventually raised the money to send a motley crew of twenty-five teenagers all the way to New Orleans.

His love of folk music eventually convinced Laliberté that he could make a career out of it. After high school he joined a folk group called La Grande Gueule (Big Mouth), with whom he played the harmonica, the accordion, and sang. Hitchhiking to gigs all over the province, he says, gave him his first taste of the performer's life. It was a constant struggle. In between gigs, he busked on the street, sometimes just in order to raise enough for his next meal. He hung around a band of street performers, jugglers, acrobats, and fire-breathers, who taught him some of the tricks of their trade.

Before I was a journalist I was a busker, who, like Guy, plied my trade on the streets of Quebec for many years. Street performing was often seen by many Quebecers as little better than panhandling. You were sometimes lucky to make three dollars in an hour, as people often thought a dime or a quarter was a sufficient tip for somebody forced to pass their hat to earn their living. But every Quebec busker had heard that there was a place where street performers were considered true artists, where one could earn a comfortable living performing on the streets—sometimes as much as $10,000 in one summer. Every Quebec busker vowed to travel to Europe to practise their trade, even if few ever got there.

When Laliberté heard the stories of the money to be made on the streets of Europe, he decided to go there and try it for himself. And when Guy Laliberté wanted something, he usually made it happen. He later described himself to a British journalist as "a dreamer, fascinated by the cultures of the world."

In 1978, he flew to London's Heathrow airport with less than $1,000 in his pocket, along with an accordion, a harmonica, a Jew's harp, and a set of musical spoons. Determined to conserve his savings until he discovered whether he could actually make money busking, his spent his first night sleeping on a bench in Hyde Park.

The first time I heard this story about him, it resonated in me. I, too, had flown to London to busk and spent my first night sleeping in Hyde Park. Although in my particular case, the association had happy memories. When I woke up in the park the next morning, I met the American actress Ava Gardner as she walked her dogs. We started talking about music, and the next thing I knew she had invited me up to her nearby condominium, where she told me fascinating stories of her marriages and relationships with a number of prominent musicians. She told me about her marriage to Frank Sinatra, whom she said was responsible for the scar she showed me on her face, where she claimed he had struck her viciously. In fact, she told me she was living in England because Sinatra's people had warned her to stay away from America after she left him. It was the beginning of a long friendship between Ava and me, which lasted until she died years later.

Laliberté's night sleeping in the park, however, wasn't as productive, thought it did have a lasting influence. It was then that he decided he didn't enjoy roughing it. The next time he visited London, with Cirque du Soleil, he stayed in an $800-a-night hotel overlooking the same park.

His English was not very proficient, which proved a liability for a busker in London, so Laliberté took the ferry and train to Paris. It was a city that he had always dreamed of visiting, as did many young Quebecers. Paris had a rich busking tradition dating back to the French revolution, when musicians would play for the large crowds waiting to watch the beheadings of French aristocracy and then pass their hats.

When I busked in Paris, I heard one of my favourite stories about street performers. It is about an infamous nineteenth century Parisian street performer named Joseph Pujol. He discovered a unique talent at a young age: he could fart at will, loudly and musically. He decided to capitalize on these abilities and took to the streets, farting the Marsellaise and other songs for the crowds and setting his farts on fire. Both acts brought him large sums of money; the crowds filled his hat with francs. Eventually, a promoter offered him a regular stage act, and Pujol became known as Le Pétomane, one of the most popular performers on the continent. His performances were enjoyed by most of Europe's royalty.

While he busked at Paris's Centre Georges Pompidou, playing Quebec folk music and telling stories for the crowds of tourists, Laliberté never enjoyed the success of Joseph Pujol. But he did have a great time and vowed to return the following summer. This, however, would not quite work out as planned.

3 With the magnet of his sheer hope and desire, Laliberté surrounded himself with the right people to get his start in show business. As he wowed people with his amazing fire breathing and juggling, he dispensed with any need for proper schooling. Laliberté learned on the streets. It is there that he learned to build a mould that would contain the shapelessness of people's psyches. His greatest skill from early on was looking people right in the eye and quickly entering into their moods and intentions.

"I've never met anyone as sharp as Guy," U2 lead singer Bono would say many years later. "He's one of the most powerful people ever in show business for a reason. He's likeable, smart, and very open to new things."

In the summer of 1980, Laliberté was ready to start using his power to work the crowds as a comet of charisma. He spent the summer in Baie-Saint-Paul working with the touring stilt-walker troupe Les Échassiers. The group failed to turn a profit, but Laliberté made his mark.

"Guy was one of the youngest performers around back then," says

Élise Lapointe, a volunteer for Les Échassiers. "You could tell from early on how much of a warrior he was. Not only was he talented, he was as sharp as a razor. He had his own vision, and I knew it would be only a matter of time before he executed it. He seemed to have no limitations. If someone asked him to jump, he would show them how high he could do it."

Lapointe says Laliberté's manners were charming, yet non-deferential. "Guy certainly did not resort to the tactics of idle chat. He was too distracted to even obey the formal logic of small talk."

After the summer tour, Guy decided to jet off to the sun, sand, and breathtaking scenery of Hawaii. While being exposed to some of the most scenic natural wonders of the world, he found the Zen-like feeling that would draw him back for the rest of his life. He was taken in by Hawaii's natural beauty, from the relaxation and tranquility of Maui to the hustle and bustle of Oahu. "Hawaii is my dream place to live," he would say years later. "It's the place where I feel most comfortable to get away from it all."

When he returned to Quebec in the late spring of 1981, Laliberté sensed an obligation to use his experiences abroad to further Quebec culture. He was a young hippie who strongly believed in the province's future, and he felt compelled to give back. He wanted to be a role model for other performers and producers and realized that his fortune in being able to travel to places like Hawaii should be turned to good use.

"Travelling the world at a young age helped Guy understand what he needed to do to realize his dreams," says a long-time friend who wishes to remain anonymous. "He loved Quebec more than anywhere else. He was determined to use his new found world knowledge to make him a success in his home province.

"His confidence had increased, and he felt like he was riding the top of his wave. Whatever might come his way, he decided that failure would not be an option. The only thing he would not tolerate was being surrounded by phonies. The wisdom he gained travelling abroad made it easy for him to spit phonies out faster than watermelon seeds."

"When he first started out," continues the friend, "he often complained that he wasn't getting the proper support. But as time went on he learned that the most important thing was to take baby steps towards his vision. No one I have ever met was able to map out strategy, with all the key steps, the way Guy did. He was a tenacious and brilliant strategist from the time he was seven years old, which is when I first met him."

That summer, Laliberté returned to Baie-Saint-Paul to start a province-wide tour with Les Échassiers. Not only was he performing again, this time he'd been appointed tour manager. Serge Roy, a respected artist with Les Échassiers, thought Laliberté was ahead of his time. "He was a man of action, someone who knocked on doors," he told journalist Tony Babinski.

A long-time resident of Baie-Saint-Paul, Gérard Mathieu, remembers meeting Laliberté at a local bar that summer. "He was the nicest person you could ever meet," Mathieu says. "When you talked to him, he made you feel as if you were the most important person in the world."

Les Échassiers were motivated by politics as much as they were by performance art. The troupe was predominantly in favour of making Quebec an independent country, with French as the official language. Only a short time earlier, in 1976, the Parti Québecois—a party of French-Canadian nationalists formed in 1970—had won the provincial elections under the leadership of René Lévesque. Levesque's government subsequently launched a series of language and cultural reforms that discouraged the use of English, causing thousands of the province's anglophones and their businesses to leave abruptly.

When, in 1980, the "yes" (pro-separatist) faction in a Quebec referendum on national sovereignty won only forty percent of the vote, many people associated with Les Échassiers were not pleased. They yearned for an alternative culture that they could call their own.

"Back in those days, most of us were hard—core separatists," says Jean Vincent, a long-time street performer from Limoilou, a borough of Quebec City. "Guy was no exception. Although he's never been outspoken about it all, I definitely remember him voicing support for the Parti Québecois. He certainly was a proponent for change, although perhaps not as radical as some of the other people who were involved in Les Échassiers. We were all real Québecois hippies; anything dealing with peace, love, and change we'd support with open arms. I don't remember any one of us who didn't wear the fleur-de-lis on his or her back.

"We desperately wanted our own identity, our own country. A lot of us became resentful of English Canada because we felt they were standing in our way. In fact, we used to call them '*les maudits Anglais*' (the damn English). We felt shamed by the way most of the English treated us. They had little respect and little curiosity about our culture; most of the English people I knew back then barely spoke a word of French.

"If you didn't speak English to them, they wouldn't give you the time of day. Street performers had a big sensitivity to this. We were treated like bums by most people in the province, both French and English. Therefore, we felt we had nothing to lose by supporting separation. Change was what we felt we needed, since things couldn't get much worse."

* * *

In 1982, Laliberté met up with Serge Roy and Robert Lagueux, who were instrumental in launching the summer festival called La Fête Foraine in Baie-Saint-Paul. Lagueux would later go on to play a key role in helping Laliberté realize his ultimate goal of creating his own business. Gilles Ste-Croix was in charge of the festival, and his infamous troupe, Le Club des Talon Hauts (the High Heels Club), was central in kicking off the inaugural event. Its group of jugglers, mimes, stilt walkers, and fire-eaters roamed the streets of the tiny village, gathering people to attend the shows.

Street performers from all over the world descended on Baie-Saint-Paul, a small town of 7,000 people. Spectators also flocked to the festival in droves and got their first view of the unique performance-art troupe. A tent was erected in a parking lot beside the town church, and although admission was free, patrons were asked to contribute a dollar for each performance they watched.

"It was worth every penny and more," says Gaston Charbonneau, a mechanic from Victoriaville who attended the festival in order to nurture his own pre-marriage dream to be a circus clown. "Looking back," he recalls, "I see I was a witness to the making of history. The talent at the festival was incredible. Never again will we see anything like it. The combination of mime, acrobatics, and music was incredibly unique. I remember at the first show I saw, I kept thinking to myself how proud I was to be a Quebecer. The next day I went to a tattoo parlour and got the phrase *Vive le Québec!* written right across my chest. And I've never had it removed." Charbonneau is now in his late fifties.

In addition to the festival, other events took place that weekend. A free concert by some of Quebec's up and coming political artists took place, an event the media referred to as a mini-Woodstock. Thousands of people materialized for a dizzying weekend of performance art and music with plenty of beer, pot, and sex. One of the foundations of La Fête Foiraine was the flagrant use of illegal substances; marijuana and LSD were the drugs of choice.

"It was hard to find anyone who wasn't tripping back then," says Pierre Piché, who drove hundreds of miles from his hometown of Aylmer to attend. "It united everyone. There were no limits. The authorities agreed to give us our space and to back off. Tolerance was the key word; you could do just about anything and get away with it. We all felt as if nothing could stop us."

Laliberté, a slim, good-looking twenty-two-year-old with long blonde hair, had a surprising edge on most of the other people associated with the festival—he had the support of his parents. He came from a middle-class family; his father Gaston and his mother Blandine, who acted as Laliberté's personal fashion consultant for his performances, used whatever resources they had to help their youngest son.

"My parents were my guiding force," Laliberté has often said. "They were always there for me. Without them I would have never achieved success. I was very fortunate to have them support me."

The festival's closing performance that year is often referred to as the prototypical version of Cirque du Soleil. Dozens of clowns, jugglers, musicians, and mimes performed onstage together. One of the musicians present was René Dupéré, a musician/composer who would go on to work with Laliberté for decades to come. At the festival Dupéré gave music lessons to youth when his group La Fanfonie was not onstage. "There had been nothing like it ever before in Quebec," he says. "It is a moment in all our lives that we'll certainly never forget."

The end-of-festival party made for one big bash, even for Laliberté, who in later years became notorious for his wild parties filled with drugs and excess.

"It was all wild," Rachel Jean, a volunteer says. "Everyone was into the sex, drugs, and innocent fun. Even though I worked for free, it was the best time I ever had. I slept with five people that weekend—three men and two women. My friend who helped organize it slept with six people, three of whom I slept with. We were all stoned. A clown was dealing the best acid you could imagine, and one of the musicians had a stack of Moroccan hash that was so popular, we ran out of it on the first afternoon. He had to call a friend to drive up from Montreal with another trunk-full. It made Woodstock look like a children's birthday party. Everyone partied like it was the last day of their life."

While the inaugural festival was highly acclaimed by both the public and the media, the artists organizing it turned out to be wretched accountants. Unforeseen expenses left the organization more than $10,000 in the red. Laliberté took the lead in trying to dig a way out of the debt; he was the only person capable of doing the math and figuring out how to turn things around. He spent the rest of the year convincing the festival team to position the event more strongly the following summer. They would need to spend more money on marketing and replace several acts with more seasoned performers. The next year, he imposed a one dollar admission fee, and as the festival progressed he promised to increase the fee to five dollars.

Even though the government did not contribute any funding, things started to turn around. Near physical exhaustion, Laliberté worked harder than ever to make the festival a success, and attendance the following year more than doubled. No one has ever disagreed that the second edition of the festival might never have taken place without his sharp business sense. Laliberté's vision showed boundless possibilities. It would be his springboard toward great things.

Through his experiences with the festival, Laliberté demonstrated a strong aptitude for mixing business with art. Many people who knew him back then recall how relentless a worker he was. A long-time friend says Laliberté practically lived on coffee and aspirin.

"He never slept. He had a dream and he lived it twenty-four hours a day. He was so raunchy, so dazzling, so daring; nothing ever seemed to faze him. Everyone was in awe of how he operated. He certainly was not a talentless person daydreaming of a great career. He had a combination of leadership and originality that was very rare. In fact, I don't think many people had ever seen anything like it before. It seemed as if he were preparing for his one big triumphant scene."

Laliberté's rallying cry to everyone around him was his confidence. He was himself an affirmation that could inspire a lost artist's dreams. He preached that success and deserving to win come from a belief in oneself and from moral wherewithal. Perhaps his own biggest virtue was shooting straight. In business, Laliberté has often said, ambiguity poisons more than betrayal.

"Ever since I've known Guy, if there is something that is bothering him, he'll say it right to your face," a former Cirque du Soleil executive says. "Love him or hate him, no one ever accused him of being a phony. He loves to talk, but never behind anybody's back."

* * *

Meanwhile, another entertainment enterprise was fighting for its life. Le Cirq, launched in 1982 by visionary artistic director Michel Laurin, had employed artists like Laliberté and Gilles Ste-Croix. Le Cirq is sometimes cited as the prime inspiration for Laliberté's own Cirque du Soleil, which would be created a couple of years later. The young Laurin had already invested his blood, sweat, and tears in the launch of his circus, and now it was in need of some capital.

By 1983, Laurin's circus was one of three in Quebec to lobby the provincial government for funding. In fact, some claim that Laurin might have been the one to catapult to fame and fortune had he received the nearly one-million-dollar government grant he applied for. Without a subsidy, it was only a matter of time before his money would run out, and in 1985 Laurin was so close to pennilessness that he had to sell his tent. It took him a year to pay off his debts and get himself back on his feet. By all accounts, Laurin the entrepreneur gambled with his heart rather than with his head.

"Laurin really didn't know how to run a business," says Stéphane Boyer, a Quebec freelance journalist who closely followed the careers of both Laurin and Laliberté. "Laurin was more into it for the passion. He had a huge ego and was power hungry. Not to say that Laliberté wasn't the same. The difference was that Laliberté was better at positioning things properly and had the ability to rise in the world when things got rough. He never took no for an answer."

The success in Baie-Saint-Paul had convinced Laliberté and Ste-Croix that there might be a bigger market out there. They began to craft a vision. They would create a travelling circus. Laliberté had always been fascinated by Gypsies; he loved their traditional livlihood of dancing and singing and playing musical instruments. Laliberté was determined to lead a similar itinerant lifestyle, but with a much broader range of entertainers at hand. The idea had big money-making potential

Laliberté worked at his goal without backing down. He exuded a kind of driven selflessness; one might even say a kind of saintliness accompanied him as he followed his direction. He was bold enough to keep to a course that most of his practical friends considered madness.

"Many people were naysayers," Stéphane Boyer says. "They didn't believe Guy would succeed, because they had no vision themselves When Guy talked of his world vision, people thought he was nuts.

They thought he was talking out of his ass. In fact, I'd say there were very few in the beginning who believed in him. They looked at him as a street performer who thought he had a shot at making it big, and they thought it highly unlikely. But how many street performers do you know who have gone on to become filthy rich?" Enough said.

4 Laliberté understands the conventional wisdom that there is always something to learn from failure. He likes to learn from other people's mistakes. By closely monitoring the failures of Michel Laurin's Le Cirq, Laliberté saw that resiliency would help him through the potholes, wrong turns, and detours ahead on the bumpy road to success.

Jacques Robert has worked all his life in circuses as a technician. He claims Laliberté was far from the first person attempting to resuscitate the allure of the circus.

"So many people tried it before Guy, but they failed," Robert says. "I'm sure Guy will be the first person to admit that he let other people go first, watched them fall, and then learned from their mistakes. Actually, it's a very smart business strategy; the risk is much less. Many of the world's most successful people did it the same way."

By 1984, Laliberté's name was becoming synonymous with the

hustle and money of producing live performance art. He had earned a reputation as a shrewd deal-maker, but his biggest challenge was just now arriving.

Quebec and the rest of Canada were planning massive celebrations for the four hundred and fiftieth anniversary of French explorer Jacques Cartier's arrival in Canada. Millions of people from all over the world were expected to descend on the province to take in the sixty-three days filled with special events and celebrations. Quebec braced itself for its biggest international event since hosting the 1976 Olympic Games. Although those games had brought world exposure to Montreal, they left both the city and province shouldering a huge deficit. This time around, event planners were going to exercise due diligence and intended to monitor every penny of their multi-million dollar budget.

When the Quebec government announced special funding for arts groups to perform at the celebrations, Laliberté, Robert Lagueux, and the rest of Le Club des Talons Hauts saw a golden opportunity to take their enterprise to the next level. But, Laliberté encountered a major obstacle. Quebec's minister of culture, Clément Richard, was lukewarm to their application. He wasn't convinced Quebecers would react favorably to such an alternative act. He said it was too different, too outside the norm. Laliberté refused to give up; he called every politician and business person he knew in the community and begged them to put pressure on the government to reconsider his application.

The organizer behind the anniversary celebrations was Gilles Loiselle, an affirmative and well-connected visionary. He had a different opinion on the matter and got behind Laliberté and Lagueux. He had followed their summer hits at La Fête Foraine and thought this unique concept would capture the hearts of all Quebecers.

Incredibly, the only other ear Laliberté found sympathetic to his rallying was that of the most powerful person in Quebec, Prime Minister René Lévesque. One of the most charismatic and well-liked politicians ever in Quebec, Lévesque shaped the province's political and social fabric forever with his unforgettable acceptance speech after sweeping the 1976 elections, when he said, "I never thought that I could be so proud to be a Quebecer."

Aside from being a master politician, Lévesque had a reputation for being able to charm women better than anyone. This is one character trait he shared with Laliberté, who would, later on, become a notorious playboy himself. It often got Lévesque into hot water with fellow politicians and the public, who were concerned he was spending more time wining and dining ladies than governing the province. Interestingly, it was Lévesque's uncanny ability to woo young women that probably sealed the deal for Laliberté.

This was the era of politics when leaders in office could more easily get the Monica Lewinsky treatment behind their wives' backs. Lévesque's Lewinsky was Amadou, a beautiful trampolinist with whom he had a prolonged clandestine affair. When Lévesque was first approached with the Laliberté proposal for the anniversary celebrations, the first person the politician consulted was Amadou. He called her immediately and asked her for her opinion.

In her first-ever public interview about her dalliance with Lévesque, Amadou told me, "René and I were passionate about a lot of the same things. We both loved to live life to its fullest."

Amadou, like many performance artists, did not live a monogamous lifestyle and had dated or slept with several performers in Laliberté's troupe while she was dating Lévesque. "Back then everyone was sleeping with everyone," she told me. "Marriage was really only the act of buying a wedding ring and having kids."

She was a big supporter of what Laliberté was trying to achieve artistically. She told Lévesque he'd be crazy not to support such an original concept. Laliberté's circus, she told Levesque, would be the most dynamic and popular attraction of the festival. Lévesque concurred. Amadou's prediction could not have been more precise. With a grant of $1.4 million, Laliberté's newly named Cirque du Soleil troupe was booked to present their show in eleven different cities in Quebec.

Laliberté maintains he named it Cirque du Soleil because his most creative ideas come when the sun shines. "Guy worships the sun as if it's his god," a long-time Cirque du Soleil employee says. "When the sun comes out, Guy loves to soak it up. It makes him feel good and it brings out his creative spirit. Some of his best ideas have been conceived under the glare of a hot summer sun. It's as if he lives just to walk around shirtless, tanned, and wearing sandals. I've known him for years, and that's how he likes to be, no matter how much money he makes. It makes him feel totally free and secure."

After celebrating the financing agreement, Laliberté and Lagueux quickly rolled up their sleeves and went to work. The first thing they needed to do was put a skilled team in place. They hired technical director Guy St-Amour, stage manager Jean David, and put Daniel Gauthier in charge of finance. Laliberté wore the title of director, while Lagueux was in charge of marketing, and Gilles Ste-Croix was hired to perform.

"It was a very tight-knit network," a former Cirque executive says. "Guy made sure everyone was taken care of and that the infrastructure was rock solid. Sure, along the way there were lots of problems and tensions. But they knew how to resolve it behind closed doors, which was the key to making things work."

A lot of bumps appeared for Laliberté and company before the first performance took place. Their signature tent, which Laliberté had had made in Italy, got damaged during a heavy rainstorm in Sainte-

Thérèse, the small town north of Montreal where rehearsals were held. There was no way it could be repaired for opening night. They made plans to use an alternative tent which would be supplied by the federal government, but this was something that Laliberté tried hard to avoid. His first shows were to take place in the heart of Quebec separatism, in the Gaspé, and the last thing he wanted was for them to happen under a tent bearing the Canadian flag. Laliberté and his staff were concerned.

"Can you imagine? After all that hard work their signature tent would not be up for opening night. Nothing else could have gone worse," says Paul Lemieux, a Quebec artisan who followed Cirque on tour for years, selling his handmade jewellery outside their shows. "I'm sure a lot of the performers were not amused. I don't think many people in Cirque at that time were into the red and white of the maple leaf. They preferred the blue and white of the fleur-de-lis."

Performers complained of the long work hours and low pay, a criticism repeatedly targeted at Laliberté over the years. "It was being like in army boot camp," recalls an old Cirque crew member. "Because we didn't have many resources back then, we had to do everything on a tight budget. Performers, crew, and even the people running the show were often reduced to tears. It was extremely stressful and emotionally exhausting."

Finally, the first show took place on June 16, 1984, in the breathtaking Gaspé region of Quebec. That day, Laliberté instructed a legion of clowns, acrobats, and musicians to parade around the small town shouting out, "The circus is in town, the circus is in town!" It was a marketing strategy reminiscent of the old-style town crier, one that would prove effective for Cirque in the early days. Despite numerous technical glitches, opening night was a hit. An instant buzz about Cirque circulated across the province. Laliberté was ever more convinced that he had a star show; his biggest problem now was that he didn't have enough tickets to sell.

The Cirque embarked on a nearly three-month tour of eleven cities. More than 30,000 spectators attended. Often, more than 5,000 people would line up for the 800 seats available. The show was different every night, which was part of Laliberté's vision. He didn't want to produce an event in which the artists would perform like robots. He wanted to keep the show fresh by introducing new routines and new sequences in every performance.

In one of the province's busiest summers ever, including nothing less than a concert by Michael Jackson at Montreal's Olympic Stadium, Laliberté finally saw his early dream come to fruition. By the end of the season, Cirque du Soleil had become a household name in Quebec. It was, by far, the most successful show of the 450th-anniversary celebrations.

"By that time Guy had become close pals with everyone in Lévesque's inner circle," a former executive of Cirque du Soleil says. "Guy was a master networker. He gave circus tickets to everyone he thought he could use for future purposes; he treated them like kings. He knew it would be well worth it down the line, and he turned out to be right. The government had no choice but to support his circus; they would have looked like fools if they didn't. Nothing else in Quebec was bringing the province so much attention." Now, the biggest question for Laliberté was how to take this success to a grander level.

To this day Laliberte credits Levesque as being the person most responsible for Cirque's survival. If not for Levesque's dedicated participation in raising the seed fuunding to launch Cirque, Laliberte acknowledges that he might be doing else today.

"Without Levesque there would be no Cirque," one of Laliberte's close friends said. "Guy is most respectful and thankful how Rene Levesque helped him. In fact I've heard Guy say many times that if not for Levesque's enthusiasm Guy would probably be still roaming around the world performing on the streets."

Lévesque's ex-lover said Quebec's premier used the Cirque as an experiment to prove to the rest of Canada and to the world that Quebec could be independent without the aid of Canada.

"He loved Laliberté's global vision and decided to show everyone that a group of young radicals from Quebec could conquer the world without needing Canada," she said. "If that happened, it would be Lévesque's way of proving to the world that Québec as an independent country could survive nicely without Canada."

Unfortunately for Lévesque, the next year, 1985, he lost the provincial election to Robert Bourassa. "If he would have won that key election in '85, Quebec most likely would be an independent country today," she said. "Once the Cirque succeeded, Lévesque would have had the right ammunition to convince the world that it was possible for Québec to be strong as an independent force."

While Cirque du Soleil will worship Levesque's role as a strong visionary and initiator forever, many people in Cirque display huge outrage and ambivalence when the name of another legendary Quebec politician's name is brought up—Robert Bourassa. Bourassa, a longtime Cirque executive said, did everything in his power to make Cirque's life miserable when he returned from political exile and ousted Levesque from office in 1985. Bourassa, the source said, kept threatening to levy higher taxes and stricter regulations on successful arts groups like Cirque because he feared they were becoming "a big political threat." Unlike Levesque, Bourassa did not have a taste for pursuing virtuous ends in the arts with personal sacrifice and put himself under the risk of public excoriation. Bourassa, the former Cirque executive said, wavered from his commitment to support Cirque and was "a total traitor." Ironically, when Bourassa lost to Rene Levesque in 1976 in what was widely viewed as the province's most embarrassing political defeat ever, he was described by a Liberal party colleague as "the most hated man in Quebec".

"He was not only the most hated man in Quebec but also the most deceitful human being on the planet," the former Cirque executive said. "Obviously, he had it in for Cirque because most of the people who founded Cirque were staunch separatists. Once Cirque started becoming successful Bourassa did everything he could to make Cirque's life miserable because he started seeing Cirque as a threat to Canada. He was also extremely jealous of how popular Levesque was with us and how Levesque helped out Cirque from the very beginning. A friend of mine who knew him well said that he once called us 'a bunch of communist stoners who are more dangerous than the FLQ.' When Bourassa came back to political power most people at Cirque prayed for his demise. We were aware that he was intent on ruining us in a very subtle way. He pretended to support us but deep down he was our enemy."

5 By early 1985, Laliberté was devising a plan to expand h is business and reach a broader audience. He decided he wo uld bring Cirque du Soleil to the rest of Canada and t hat federal funding would help him do it. He also knew that he need ed to surround himself with skilled people. The one person Laliberté increa singly relied upon to move things along was Daniel Gauthier, the person he had placed in charge of handling Cirque's financial books. Gauthier an d Laliberté's history goes back to when they atten ded grade school together in their hometown of Saint-Bruno, an off-island suburb of Montreal.

Born on September 5, 1958, Gauthier was handsome but undistinguished; his long hair and unkempt appearance made him look more like a Beatles roadie than an accountant. His cheeks were usually unshaven, and he dressed casually in old jeans and badly fitting shirts. The unending challenge at which he always toiled was how to make money with Cirque du Soleil. It would take years for him to figure it out, but Laliberté was patient with Gauthier, as he usually was with the people he put in key positions.

In 1981, Gauthier had struck up a friendship with Gilles Ste-Croix on the steps of Le Balcon Vert in Baie-Saint-Paul. The two had talked at length about Laliberté and the burgeoning arts scene in the summer town. It was the start of what would become a long business relationship and love-hate triangle between the three.

"Without Gauthier, I don't think Cirque du Soleil would have made it through those early days," a former executive at Cirque says. "Guy was an idealist with a vision to conquer the world. He enjoyed drinking champagne on a beer budget. That was the way he liked to live. Gauthier was completely the opposite; he was much less extravagant. He was able to balance out Guy, who liked to spend money like there was no tomorrow."

Gauthier was a formidable numbers person who understood economics better than anyone else Laliberté knew. He was also the only one of the gang who had any idea how to use a computer. He'd spend hours on end carefully tallying the Cirque du Soleil balance sheet. The key to running a successful business, Gauthier believed, was to not spend what you didn't have. Laliberté was the total opposite. This resulted in the pair squaring off about excessive spending on a near-daily basis. To this day, many credit Gauthier's analysis and implementation as the key ingredients in Cirque's financial success.

"There used to be fireworks between those two," a former Cirque executive confides. ''They worked the same way a car does: Guy was the gas; Daniel, the brakes. But without Daniel I don't think Guy would have gone so far. Many companies have a great vision, but they don't know how to run things properly and end up going bust. Daniel saved Cirque from this kind of financial disaster.

"They were both having fun living out their dreams. I remember seeing them in their tiny offices back then, looking like kids in a candy store for the first time. It was beautiful to see two young Quebecers with such passion and vision and determination. I don't think anyone has or ever will again see anything like this pair. They were unique."

A lot of the media attention showered on Cirque du Soleil in the early days focused on the same theme: the Cirque used no animals. Whenever the subject came up, Laliberté usually responded, "We'd rather employ a bunch of Canadian acrobats than a bunch of American elephants." There was no shortage of documentation about animal cruelty in the training of performing animals, and animal rights activists around the world praised Laliberté. Cirque du Soleil was a breath of fresh air.

Many people mistakenly believe that Cirque was the first circus to not use animals. But *cirque nouveau*, or contemporary circus, is a performing arts movement born in the 1970s that does not use animals. In *cirque nouveau*, story and theme are conveyed by jugglers, acrobats, and trapeze artists who perform with atmospheric music and stunning aerial silks. Dozens of such circuses sprang up in different parts of the world, long before Guy Laliberté and Cirque du Soleil arrived on the scene. Circus Oz in Australia and the Pickle Family Circus in San Francisco had similarities with Cirque du Soleil. The greatest difference is that they didn't have a savvy businessman like Guy Laliberté to position them properly.

"With all due respect to Cirque du Soleil, they were not inventing the wheel," says Ellen Goodis, a juggler and occasional acrobat who performed in Circus Oz. Goodis, who today works as a fitness consultant in New York, was amazed by how much attention Cirque du Soleil got for not using animals.

"It had been done before all over the world. Really, I never understood what all the big fuss was about. They must have spent a lot on media and marketing. I always thought it wasn't fair how people credited them for being the first circus not to use animals, when in fact it had been done by many others years before they even came along."

Yet Laliberté never claimed he didn't use animals out of a concern for their welfare. He admitted, like most other *cirque nouveau* owners, that it was more about the financial welfare of Cirque du Soleil.

"Most of these people put up circuses without animals because it was cheaper to employ humans," Goodis says. "I don't think Laliberté or anyone else was concerned about the atrocious conditions animals had been exposed to for so many years in old-style circuses. In fact if we look now at how it all played out, a lot of the humans in these circuses were treated worse than the animals in the old circuses! Who would ever have thought it would turn out that way?"

* * *

To prepare the ground for a tour in English Canada, Laliberté asked his stage manager, Jean David, to give a key interview for CBC national radio. There was one problem with this strategy: David could barely say "Happy Birthday" in English, let alone carry on the kind of lengthy interview that Laliberté was banking on to help fill seats. Fortunately, the radio host was sympathetic to David's sparse English and made the interview humorous more than anything. It worked wonders, and with his broken English David endeared himself to thousands of English radio listeners. Cirque was now making waves across the country.

Meanwhile, as rehearsals intensified, several Cirque performers began to burn out. A dank hostility seeped from them due to the low pay and long work hours Laliberté imposed. Some of the veteran performers went weak at the thought of doing a full scale cross-Canada tour. Things were getting too intense.

This led to the beginning of a major problem that would plague Cirque for years. Drug addiction, for many of the company's top performers, was a response to the intensity of Cirque life. The drugs of choice were not just pot and alcohol; the abuse of substances like cocaine, LSD, and heroin became prevalent.

Laliberté was all too aware but turned a blind eye. He would watch rehearsals without a quiver of emotion, and then in the silence that followed the performers' discussions, he would begin to speak. He could talk for two hours about a scene that had taken five minutes. He could go on for another hour if the subject was worthy of analysis, knowing all the while that half his performers were strung out on heavy drugs. He would do nothing about it because the last thing he wanted was to be accused of hypocrisy. He was no angel; he smoked pot and snorted the occasional line of cocaine. In later years, as we will see further along in Laliberté's story, his appetite for drugs intensified, as did the atrocious drug habits of many others involved in the Cirque.

"It's amazing that some of the performers didn't pass out or die during a performance," recounts a former Cirque clown who asked to be identified as "Jacques". "There was plenty of white powder and plenty of brown powder around the circus. I saw people injecting, smoking, and snorting right on site. I was no angel either; I used to snort lines of coke each day in the bathroom before rehearsal would begin. It's amazing I'm still alive. It's amazing any of us are. We partied just as hard as we practised. We needed it to get by. Life in Cirque du Soleil was not glamorous at all; it was very difficult work. Drugs gave us the relief we needed."

When performers become depressed and lackluster, the audience will notice. This was likely another primary reason for the mixed audience—and—media reaction to that first English tour. No one can ever estimate the damages drug use must have done to Cirque during these early days.

"Guy learned on that tour some of the biggest lessons of his entire life," a former Cirque member says. "When he got back to Montreal, he realized changes had to be made if he was going to take it to the next level. He saw that a lot of the people on tour were more interested in partying than performing. Everyone, from performers to technical crew, was whooping it up much more than he had anticipated. He knew this was something that could jeopardize the future of the Cirque."

\* \* \*

The Canadian tour kicked off in mid-May with one month of performances in Montreal before continuing to Sherbrooke, Quebec city, and then to Ottawa, Toronto, and Niagara Falls in Ontario. When the English Canada part of the itinerary got underway, the tour was received with an unexplainable and disappointing lack of excitement. Unlike at home, many of the shows were half empty. Cirque started losing money fast, as Laliberté started to realize they hadn't done enough marketing.

He could have simply cancelled the rest of the tour after Ottawa, but he understood that the bad publicity he would receive by cancelling would cost him any future chance of conquering English Canada. By fierce determination and creative marketing on the part of Laliberté and Gauthier, they were able to turn things around. Even if many in English Canada were unfamiliar with the Cirque's Québecois performers, talented favourites like Gilles Ste-Croix, dancing the tango on stilts around the town and in the circus ring, wowed the audiences.

In fact, Laliberté's choice of resources was crucial. He showed unwavering confidence in the capabilities of the man he had hired to put the touring show together in only fifteen days. That man was Franco Dragone. Dragone had been recommended by Guy Caron, founder of the École de Cirque in Montreal, where Dragone was directing a production. Caron convinced Laliberté that Dragone's history of success in parts of Europe would be valuable to the Cirque. This would certainly turn out to be true. Dragone would go on to direct pratically all of Cirque du Soleil's production's from 1985 to 1998.

Much of the talent recruited to Cirque was via Caron's circus school, which was a popular alternative to regular-curriculum schooling for many young, artsy Quebecers. Laliberté trusted Caron's artistic intuition and relied on him to groom new talent for future Cirque shows. When Caron recommended a performer, Laliberté was all ears.

In 1974, Caron had studied at one of the world's top circus schools in Budapest, where he took extensive notes on what makes a circus school work. Other future Cirque du Soleil performers attended the school at the same time. Among them were perhaps the two most popular clowns ever in Cirque de Soleil, Rodrigue Tremblay, better known as Chocolat, and Sonia Côté, who became Cirque's loveable clown Chatouille. They spent two years there learning every nuance of movement and body language that was required to be a successful clown. They also learned to juggle, play musical instruments, walk the tightrope, and sing.

"The clowns there were not supposed to be funny, so it turned out to be quite an educational experience," Caron recalled years later. "One thing for sure, the roots of Cirque du Soleil were planted in Budapest during those two years. It gave the three of us the proper experience to bring back and share with other performers who would join Cirque du Soleil."

Laliberté had hired for master of ceremonies Michel Barrette, who enamoured the English crowds with his French accent. Despite the charms of the Quebec accents to be heard at Cirque performances, however, the tour was not devoid of racist barbs toward the more francophone acts, including Les Stagiaires, Chatouille, La Ratatouille, and Denis Lacombe.

"A lot people resented the French in Quebec because they were trying to separate our country," the late Montreal journalist Ted Blackman once said. He had attended the Montreal and Ottawa shows. "Frankly, I couldn't give a damn. I just wanted to get entertainment value, which Cirque definitely offered. If they would have made a better attempt to include English in those early years, it would have definitely been more successful. For example, a friend of mine went to see them in Toronto and said people in the crowd were yelling 'fucking separatist' or 'go home, Frenchies.' With the Parti Quebecois determined to separate Quebec, it was not the best time for a francophone company to try to conquer English Canada. They had big balls, trying to do that."

When the tour ended, Cirque's finances had once again run dry. Not even another gift from Rene Lévesque to the tune of a quarter million dollars was enough to stabilize Cirque's huge debt. They were now over $750,000 in the red, and the bank was pressuring them as their debts increased. Things had never seemed bleaker.

Gauthier sat down and carefully orchestrated a plan with Laliberté. Both were worried that Cirque would go bankrupt in a flash if they couldn't come up with a solid bailout plan. They decided to turn to the Quebec business community. Local insurance mogul Claude Castonguay helped Cirque reach out to some of the province's most powerful businessmen. Cirque people practically begged on hands and knees for support. To Laliberté's delight, people responded, and investors started lining up to finance his enterprise.

Indeed, Laliberté and Gauthier were experts at getting people to listen when they talked. They often counselled their investors on money and personal problems when they became close friends with them. Everyone I interviewed for this book unanimously agreed they were drawn to Laliberté for his incredible mind.

"Guy and Daniel were two of the best-loved and respected people in Montreal," recalls Montreal businessman Allan Fortin. "Even if they had huge debts, people still wanted to do business with them because what they were doing was so cool. Guy was slightly short, but nothing was wasted on his body. He had great manners. He was one of the few people I met in show business who had class."

"One thing for sure about Guy is that he never sacrificed anything to try to save a penny," Fortin says. "He did and still does everything to the highest extreme of quality. If he can't do it that way, then he doesn't do it at all. Very few people in the world are able to live like that."

What is most interesting about studying Laliberté as he was back then is how he emitted a confidence that most people had never seen, not only in Quebec circles but beyond them as well. He clearly demonstrated that he was not afraid to take giant risks and fall down flat.

"What he showed from early on was that each time he fell off his bicycle, he immediately hopped back on and kept riding," Fortin remembers. "Most people fall off and then die. They're too afraid to get back on, from fear that they could end up losing again." Laliberté also made his mark by marching to his own rhthym. With his knowledge of street performing, Laliberté was not a typical head of a company. His idiosyncrasies from back then are still legendary.

"His mind and his approach were extremely unconventional," says Fortin. "For example, the way he mixed partying with work was considered a big no-no. Guy didn't give a damn, and the best part was that he wouldn't attempt to hide it. He'd sleep with some of the hottest women in Montreal and would answer straight up if you asked who they were and how he met them. He was quite proud of his lifestyle. Many tried hard to emulate him, but they'd burn out in a week or two. He has always been able to maintain his ferocious lifestyle without showing any signs of slowing down. It's quite amazing."

Everyday Laliberté became more single-minded in his vision of Cirque. It is fair to say he became increasingly motivated by money and power, an evolution that some of the Cirque colleagues he started out with on the streets started to resent.

"As time marched forward, you could see how Cirque's vision was changing into Guy Laliberté's vision," says the former Cirque clown, Jacques. "I know for a fact that many of the people he started out with, back when he was with Le Club Des Talons Hauts and the festival in Baie-Saint-Paul were not amused. They were mostly hippies and extreme socialists. This whole vision of trying to turn Cirque into a massive empire did not go over well with them. They were starting to accuse Guy of being a control freak, which I think he'd probably own up to. It was either Guy's way or the highway."

Laliberté's and Gauthier's exuberance began to show results by 1986, when Cirque procured several major contracts. Cirque du Soleil was among the small group of Quebec artists invited to showcase their talents at the World's Fair in Vancouver, at Expo 86. Laliberté was not going to take any chances with this tour. Franco Dragone was once again brought on board to oversee the concept of the show. He was joined by cutting-edge costume designer Michel Crête, who would give Cirque a more alternative and unique feel. Together they created *La Magie Continue*, a show that featured the original music of René Dupéré, the musician whom Laliberté had befriended back in Baie-Saint-Paul.

"It was the beginning of something totally different, something totally fresh," Jacques recalls. "After losing so much money the year before, Guy decided to take more artistic risks. He moved away from the traditional busker style circus to a show with a more structured concept, with unconventional costumes and music. It was a big risk to take, but I don't think there's a person today on the planet who would question Guy's decision. It gave shape to the circus for the next twenty-five years."

Thus began Laliberté's venture into a whole new sphere, into a sort of post-modern performance-art project. To ensure there would be no technical glitches, he sent a team of technicians to Vancouver a month before the shows to work out the logistics. *La Magie Continue* featured thirty-five performers from Quebec and other parts of the world, including France, Cambodia, Mexico, and Holland. Laliberté liked hiring people from other parts of the world because they came cheap and they gave Cirque a more exotic feel. The circus gave a series of warm-up shows and played the Vancouver Children's Theatre Festival before performing at Expo 86. There, Cirque du Soleil captured the hearts and imaginations of people visiting from all over the world.

It was an emotionally successful start to another Canadian tour. "Vancouver was pivotal," Jacques says. "If we hadn't had a good show there, Cirque du Soleil might have had to fold. We were showcasing a new concept. If the reviews had been bad, I don't think we would have had a chance to survive. It was all or nothing."

Unlike any other circus on the planet, Cirque du Soleil was reaching out to an upscale audience. Very few children attended shows. Most spectators were adults between twenty-one and forty-five, a demographic with a high amount of disposable income. This type of audience would spend money not only on tickets but also on merchandise, which would become a cash cow for Cirque. Corporate advertisers signed up quickly, including Air Canada and Hostess Chips, as Cirque exploited every avenue toward profit.

Meanwhile, Laliberté was yearning to perform more often. His recent efforts had been focused on the periphery of the circus, where he was organizing and mobilizing support and publicity. But he wanted to breathe fire again, a talent for which he was recognized as one of the best in the world. He had become accomplished at breathing fire during the year he spent in Hawaii, where it is a common feature at their legendary luaus. There was still a creative aspect to his ambition, and despite his deep commitment to running the business, he spent hours practising his daredevil fire routine.

He was not worried about making mistakes, even with the fire. Why should he be? If his blunders had hooks, they would be big enough to catch sharks. "Nothing could stop him," a former executive of Cirque du Soleil says. "He was determined to turn every situation into a positive one, no matter what it was. Not only was he ambitious, he was equally as sharp. He could smell success, and failure was never an option." He still preferred living on the edge.

6 Laliberté loves loud music. He says it drowns out all the voices in his head and keeps his demons at bay. When he wasn't rehearsing his performance with Cirque, he was cranking the stereo to maximum in his brand new Renault Fuego sports car. The Fuego was the start of a love affair with sports cars that would eventually lead him to own multiple Ferraris, BMWs, and McLarens.

While Gauthier worked round the clock trying to put Cirque back on track financially, Laliberté was busy partying on the town with his tight-knit group of Montreal hipster friends and a different hot young girl each night. He spent thousands of dollars a week paying for everyone's dinners, drinks, and "pharmaceuticals," as one close friend puts it.

"Ever since I met him twenty years ago, Guy has been the most generous person, not only with me, but with everyone around him," the longtime friend says. "He'd pay for all of us to have fun. Expensive dinners, drinks, women, and drugs were always complimentary if you were in Guy's inner circle. He loves making others happy." Most of his expenses he put through the company.

When darkness fell each night in Montreal, Laliberté shone his brightest. He used to wear pants so tight you could have read Braille through them. He was an incorrigible flirt with an ability to pick up any woman he set his sights on. One might think all his experience with women would make him indifferent to sex, but it was the complete opposite; his manner was delicate and tender, something the ladies found hard to resist.

"There was nothing I wanted more than to run off with Guy and have a drink and listen to his cute voice and fall into his bottomless eyes," confides a former girlfriend, a woman who wishes to be known as Claire. "Every time I saw him, I got goose bumps. I knew he was sleeping with lots of other women, but it didn't matter. I was head over heels about him."

Gauthier was not amused by all the spending these activities entailed. He called his old buddy Normand Latourelle, who had worked closely with Cirque in its early days. Latourelle was a man of diplomacy and respect, a man whom Gauthier was convinced might be the only person capable of talking some sense into Laliberté. According to journalist Jean Beaunoyer, Gauthier told Latourelle that Laliberté "was acting like a delinquent," and that Laliberté's extravagant lifestyle was one of the main reasons Cirque was racking up so much debt.

"Laliberté's frivolous spending put Gauthier on the verge of a nervous breakdown," a former Cirque executive explains. "Guy was living life as if he were Howard Hughes. He seemed to think money grew on trees. He was obsessed with showing everyone how much power and wealth he had by sharing it. He had so many leeches around him that he was racking up ridiculous expenses. He never said no. He treated all his friends as if they were his children and supported many people's lifestyles and habits."

Gilles Ste-Croix remained one of Laliberté's biggest allies and condemned the others for talking behind Laliberté's back. Ste-Croix and Laliberté had more in common than any of the other senior people at Cirque. They were both buskers who had made good, who chose to never forget that they came from the streets.

"No matter what, you couldn't divide those two," the former Cirque executive says. "Although they were quite different in demeanour, they shared a lot in common. Their vision was the same: carefree and intrepid. If one of them fell down, the other was usually there to fall on. It was a relationship that was fascinating. I don't think I've ever met two more dynamic people. I think if they would have been alive sixty years ago they would have been more popular than Laurel and Hardy."

Laliberté's world changed drastically toward the end of 1986 when he became severely ill with meningitis. His wild lifestyle had caught up to him. He was bedridden for weeks, and his absence left Cirque in more disarray than ever. No one knew who was in charge. Was it Daniel Gauthier? Guy Caron? Laliberté, even though he wouldn't be around for weeks? Cirque was now plagued with too many chefs standing around the broth.

"Everyone wanted to be in charge," says the former Cirque executive. "When Guy was absent, there was a scurrying by some people to take command. It was very Napoleonic. The problem was that people couldn't acknowledge that no matter how much Guy partied, there was nobody else capable of being the head honcho. All the other people were good support staff, but nobody was capable of leading Cirque the way Guy did. He was a real leader."

Recuperating at home with the aid of a few close friends who played nurse, Laliberté was pissed off to see his cohorts seemingly intent on usurping his command. He vowed to return to Cirque with more ambitious plans than ever before. The first thing he did was sit face to face with the executive branch of Cirque and outline a new strategy that he guaranteed would make Cirque a household name around the world.

He had plans to conquer the American and European markets, which had long histories of supporting circuses. He also realized the value of pouring megabucks into marketing. "We need to surround ourselves with the best marketing people in the world," he said at the time. "To make money you have to spend money. The formula is that simple."

Laliberté had a huge smile on his face by the beginning of 1987. The rest of the Canadian tour had been a huge success. Cirque had performed 206 shows to sold-out audiences in Vancouver, Sherbrooke, Montreal, Quebec City, Saint-Sauveur, Longueuil, Ottawa, and Toronto. Due to Laliberté's perseverance and a strong support staff, their large debt had been erased and Cirque was now sporting a surplus of more than $670,000.

"That tour was pivotal," recounts the former Cirque executive. "Finally, years of hard work had paid off. Now they were ready to conquer the rest of the world. It was Guy's biggest dream to create a brand name known in every corner of the world. A lot of people doubted him, but he never blinked. He had a vision, and nothing could stop him—not even his own support staff, who would have been content performing in Canada and earning a decent living rest of their lives. Guy wanted it all or nothing. That's the way he's lived every day of his life."

Laliberté decided to take the biggest risk of his career in 1987. After re-privatizing Cirque and establishing Gauthier and himself as principal owners, he set his sights on the biggest circus ring in showbiz:

Hollywood. Robert Fitzpatrick, president and founder of the Los Angeles Arts Festival, invited Cirque to be a featured act. The festival had been re-launched that year thanks to the support of L.A. Mayor Tom Bradley, the city's first African American mayor. His twenty years in office there marked the longest mayoral term ever in L.A. A couple of summers had passed since Bradley had helped bring the Olympics to his city, and he was determined to come up with a new plan to bring the tourists back.

Getting Cirque to L.A. meant overcoming bigger obstacles than ever before. The festival couldn't afford to finance Cirque; they could only offer a backend deal in which the circus would receive a percentage of gate receipts. This meant some difficulty in actually funding Cirque's transportation to the festival. Laliberté was livid, but far from discouraged. One of the guarantees that festival president Fitzpatrick had promised was the distribution of over one million flyers in the L.A. area. Laliberté, Gauthier, and Latourelle salivated over this prospect.

"They weighed it all out and went ahead and took this giant risk," the former Cirque executive says. "If they conquered L.A., the world would be on their doorstep right away. It was now or never."

Laliberté took the gamble and booked the entire production a one-way trip. Had the show been a flop, Cirque would have had to walk back to Montreal.

"The greatest business people in the world are giant risk takers," explains Dan Weisman, a California-based financial analyst. "Every person I studied who has been successful has taken giant risks— people like Bill Gates, Warren Buffett, and even politicians like President Barack Obama. Laliberté, back then, put his money where his mouth is. He put it all on the line. Those are the kind of people I consider to be real players and leaders. They're the type of people who rewrite history."

Nevertheless, Laliberté realized Cirque would need much more than a million flyers to fill seats. He instructed Latourelle, who had an incredible track record promoting top Quebec artists, to hire the biggest and most powerful public relations agency in Hollywood. After much research, Latourelle reached out to the PR firm that handled music icons Michael Jackson and Barbra Streisand. Solters, Roskin & Friedman told Latourelle that an aggressive marketing campaign for Cirque would cost $250,000. Gauthier practically fell off his chair when Latourelle told him, but Laliberté wasn't fazed. "No big deal," he told his colleagues. "If we spend $250,000 to make two million, I don't see anything wrong with it." They would find the money.

Everyone in Cirque was nervous the week the show was scheduled to open. Fewer than 3,000 tickets had been sold for its thirty-day run. It looked like Laliberté and his performers might be hitchhiking back to Montreal. Never one to run from a challenge, Laliberté had the performers out roaming the streets all week in full costume, trying to draw attention and generate ticket sales. No high-priced marketing firm could have come up with such an idea. The great question to be answered now was how effective it would be at the box office.

Perhaps the biggest thrill of Laliberté's young career was while driving in L.A. a couple of days before opening night. He noticed a billboard ahead promoting Cirque's show at the festival. He stopped his car and looked at it in near disbelief.

"The fact that he was even able to get this far was incredible," Los Angeles journalist Sherri David says. "It's not often that a guy, who just a few years back was busking for his next meal, can pull up in L.A. and see his name in lights. This might have been the first time it had ever happened. Even if there hadn't been a single ticket sold in L.A., I don't think it would be fair to call Laliberté anything else but successful."

Opening night, September 3, in the Little Tokyo area of L.A.

attracted the who's who of Hollywood, including Madonna, Michael Jackson, and Sylvester Stallone. This was Laliberté's entrance into the A-List world, a group he'd end up having at his disposal for the rest of his career. Even legendary *Tonight Show* host Johnny Carson sent out a personal invitation to Laliberté to bring several Cirque performers on his show. Jane Fonda fell in love with Cirque's unique artistic concept and took in seven performances. Hollywood had fallen in love with Cirque

*The Los Angeles Times* gave a glowing review of the show, and *USA Today* and *The New York Times* would soon follow. The media was so hot on the trail of Laliberté's enterprise that he couldn't keep up with all the media requests. There was no more fear of roughing it all the way back home. If things kept going this way, he'd be able to afford to drive the entire Cirque back to Montreal in stretch limos.

The day after opening night, L.A. was in a frenzy to buy tickets. Originally priced at $19 a ticket, scalpers were getting up to $200. In less than twenty-four hours, Cirque became the hottest ticket in town. In the end, Cirque did thirty-six shows there, after which they performed in San Diego and then Santa Monica, a kind of extension of L.A. and where they became a fixture for years to come.

"Cirque du Soleil took L.A. by storm, sort of the way the Beatles took America by storm back in 1964," says legendary American TV talk-show host, Joe Franklin. "We had never before seen anything so artistic, beautiful, and unique as Cirque. Many accuse Americans of being close-minded people, but when it comes to art, we probably have the most sophisticated taste in the world. We love the underdog, and we love discovering new art forms. Cirque du Soleil was the most unique act we saw since the Fab Four came to America. I remember covering it on my show. I called it Cirquemania, because it so reminded me of the impact Beatlemania had on all of us, decades ago."

"We're just a bunch of artistic French Canadians," Gilles Ste-Croix told a bunch of American journalists. "We're from a province of six million people and have now entered a big sea of 250 million people. We have to fight to speak French and to protect our culture. We're thrilled about our success, but we don't feel we really owe anybody anything."

Laliberté's mind began travelling and thinking at the speed of light. For the first time in his life he was in complete control of everything around him. He was in a realm of consciousness he had never imagined before, where every star wanted to be his friend.

The heads of Columbia Pictures offered him a movie deal about Cirque du Soleil. As negotiations progressed, Laliberté realized that the deal was very good—for Columbia, but not for Cirque. He'd have to forfeit too many rights to Columbia, which wanted to own everything and just pay Laliberté a fee for licensing. Before the deal was finalized, Laliberté pulled out. To this day, he cites the move as the principal reason why Cirque du Soleil remains an independent and mostly privately owned company.

"For Guy, dealing with Columbia was like going back to school," the late Montreal journalist Ted Blackman said around the time the deal fell through. "When Columbia first contacted him, he had stars in his eyes, because they're the biggest entertainment outfit in the world. But as negotiations took place, he realized they were just people like himself who were only interested in one thing: making money. He saw many more negatives than positives about signing with them. It taught him that the best person to be put in charge of his destiny was only one person—himself!"

After Laliberté backed out of the Columbia deal, word got back to him of how an executive at the studio had called him a cocky short guy, dressed like an acid head, with an ego the size of his own circus tent. Laliberté wasn't bothered in the least.

"People can call me anything they want," Laliberté told friends. "If I spent my days worrying about the names people call me, I wouldn't get any sleep. I live for my passion, and if people try to bring it down, I only wish them the best of luck. Until they succeed, I will always work hard to move forward."

Friends were worried that there was still one thing standing in Laliberté's way: his lifestyle. He was a chain smoker, heavy drinker, and frequent drug user. He told people he wanted to leave Cirque by the time he turned thirty, but at twenty-eight years old the night before the grand opening in L.A., close friends were worried that his intense lifestyle might not even let him be alive at thirty.

"I don't think there's a person alive who could keep up with him," one of his close friends says. "He was just so extreme. He told me that when he turned thirty, he'd quit Cirque to pursue another one of his lifelong dreams, to travel and explore exotic places in the world. I remember warning him that if he continued to party and work at his current pace, he might not be around in two years to make that decision. He was a walking time bomb."

7 Cirque went from being heavily in debt to being millions of dollars ahead. Much had changed in a mere eighteen months. Shows in New York were highly successful, and other American cities were begging for performances.

Laliberté's jet-set life caused a storm once again; he could be spotted driving his brand new Porsche with a different hot woman in the passenger seat almost every day, which engaged him in a major conflict with the rest of the Cirque's brass. Some of them decided to quit. Franco Dragone had already left because of a fallout with Laliberté, whom he thought was interfering with his vision as a director. Dragone, a Belgian, told friends he'd never again work with Laliberté, a vow he reneged on several times during his long-term relationship with Laliberté and Cirque.

Laliberté held his own. He knew that no person, not even himself, was indispensable. But by candidly recognizing his enemies, Laliberté took an important step to preserve his power. He left the job of revealing his inadequacies to his critics, who had a hard time shaking him up.

"If a bomb went off in his car with him in it, I think he'd come out unscathed," says a former Cirque executive. "Guy could handle almost anything. He was the most resilient person you could ever meet. The people who tried to rock his world and take over his role would be thrown out on the street in a second. Guy never tolerated backstabbing and in-house politics. He'd make sure the people who did that faced serious consequences."

The biggest conflict to escalate that year was between Laliberté and Guy Caron, the head of the circus school who was now Cirque's artistic director. They sparred for months over differences in business and artistic vision. Laliberté wanted to exploit Cirque's financial potential to the maximum, a vision that Caron opposed vehemently. He accused Laliberté of exploiting artists, of being a money-hungry businessman who would be better off selling used cars.

"Before he quit Cirque to take a post in France, Caron called Laliberté just about every bad name in the book," the former Cirque executive says. "Interestingly, the new job Caron took paid very well, over $100,000 a year. Clearly, he was jealous of what Laliberté accomplished and wanted to try to rain on Laliberté's parade. It failed miserably. Laliberté saw through his scheme and got him to leave."

Caron could not bring himself to make amends with Laliberté. Before he left he did what he could to sabotage Cirque. He convinced several key performers to leave with him. This killed any chance Laliberté had of erecting another show to complement the one already on tour.

"*Cirque Réinventé* was the name of the show on the road at that time, and it was doing extremely well," the former executive says. "Laliberté and Caron fell out the hardest when Laliberté insisted on putting another show, *Eclipse*, on the road. He wanted to make more money, and this was the perfect way. Caron was against it to the point where he left Cirque and took a lot of people with him. It caused Laliberté major headaches. He had to put *Eclipse* on the back burner."

When Caron left, Laliberté didn't show a puff of guilt. He triumphed easily over his colleague's departure and hired his old friend Gilles Ste-Croix, in February 1988, to be artistic director. Ste-Croix sensed none of the gloom that Caron had. He stood by Laliberté with affection and respect.

"Ste-Croix is often referred to as being the father of Cirque," the former executive says. "Laliberté brought him back for a reason. He wanted to put an end to the mutiny. He knew that with Ste-Croix there was no chance of a performance like Caron's. Ste-Croix never sided against Laliberté, even if he didn't always agree."

To make sense of all the chaos behind the dynamic cast of characters running Cirque, I interviewed a woman who claims she has slept with every top Cirque administrator, including Laliberté, Gauthier, and Ste-Croix. She regaled me with stories that were more Fellinieseque than anything—magic moments combined with a shocking and flamboyant realism.

Fluent in French and English, "Annie" worked in Cirque for years as an acrobat, part-time choreographer, and stand-in. One of the former Cirque executives I interviewed for this book had put me in contact with her. A stunning brunette, she gave me her life story in just over an hour. I wish she had let me video the interview because everything she said was brilliant.

Annie claims everyone running Cirque was "fucked up," some worse than others. None of them were hell-bent on fixing themselves. No matter how many years passed, she says, each member of Cirque's upper echelons seemed to go deeper and deeper into a darker world, regardless of how many millions they were making.

She says most of the "horny little boys" running Cirque had mistresses all over the world and kept getting into relationships that caused them and the Cirque major damage. She claims *les boys* shared the same goal: "to fuck as many women as they could until they dropped dead."

"They were all decent human beings until it came to women," Annie says. "Once they got you to go out for drinks with them, they became the animals that were absent in their circus. They would not take 'no' for an answer. First they tried to charm you—they were certainly most charming—and if that didn't work they'd ply you with the most expensive booze, get you stoned, and voilà, the next morning you'd wake up in their bed naked."

As for Laliberté, Annie refers to him as a "fine specimen." She adored his edge. "From the first time I laid eyes on him, I just wanted to fuck him," she says. "Anybody who's ever met Guy will agree that he's one of the most interesting people in the world. He was always very cool, almost detached. It seemed like a lot was always going on inside him, but he would keep it to himself. I knew better than to ask. No matter how many good times we had together, I had to remember he was my boss."

Annie recalls taking tango lessons with Gilles Ste-Croix. She refers to him as an irresistibly charming man. "He was the most real person I ever met," she says. "Gilles was one of the most romantic people, a real gypsy-like and passionate *voyageur*. Unlike everyone else in Cirque du Soleil's upper brass, Gilles was more concerned about the beauty of art and stretching its boundaries. Some of the best moments I had in my life were in his presence. He's an incredible man."

Annie says working for the Cirque back then was pretty unglamorous because of the hard working conditions. "That's why we were all fucking each other's brains out at night. We needed a release."

She remembers spending many nights at Laliberté's pad, partying till the next morning. She recalls one time, after a night of sex and drugs, drawing back the shades and looking out on a majestic view, yet feeling horribly sad and empty.

"The truth is, there were moments when it all got pretty sad," she says. "When the party was over, I often felt out of control and very depressed. When you first get into Cirque you're made to feel very special, anointed. Once you're inside, you become part of the family; you feel accepted and wanted. But as time goes on, you wonder if it's real. I guess we all need our illusions.

"I felt I was living my life like almost being in a cult. You could spend years there without seeing anything else. You start to think that the only way to live life is to give everything you have to Cirque—your soul, your well-being, and your body. Years later, when I look back on it, I really have no regrets. I got to travel the world, meet incredible people, and party more than most people do in a lifetime, or six lifetimes. It was a wild experience."

Annie claims some of the men who ran Cirque swung both ways. Laliberté, she insists, had surrounded himself with a lot of gay guys. But she never saw the smoking gun. At that time, however, it wasn't cool to come out of the closet.

"It wouldn't surprise me if Guy went both ways," she says. "He had a lot of gay friends and used to party at a lot of clubs in Montreal's gay village. To this day, I suspect he must have experimented, because he liked bizarre and kinky sex. He had a creative sexual mind. But I never saw the proof. There were rumours, but until someone shows me photos of Guy in bed with another guy, I'll reserve judgment.

"One guy in particular whom I slept with many times was definitely screwing some of the male clowns on the side," she says. "A lot of people in Cirque were gay. They just kept it to themselves because it wasn't like it is today; people were afraid to come out. But we all knew who was straight and who was gay. We knew everything about everyone; that's how close we all were."

As for drugs, Annie claims that there were so many drugs around Cirque that it could have been called the biggest pharmaceutical operation in Quebec. "Whatever your drug of choice was, there would be a clown, a technician, or a performer who would be able to supply it," she says. Laliberté was very generous with his drugs, mostly pot and cocaine, but while "the guys running Cirque were certainly into drugs, they weren't the ones dealing them. You had to get your stash from one of the crew members or performers. They'd have the best drugs because the best dealers in town became aware that almost everyone in Cirque had a habit. We were all completely out of our minds back then."

She's amazed that so many performers were able to carry out their audacious circus acts stoned. She explains that backstage before a show, while the audience was piling into the tent, people were running around like crazy—half-naked, excited, and stoned out of their minds. She claims she'd often grab a hot guy, a technician or performer, find a private changing space, lift up her skirt, and fuck his brains out minutes before the curtain was raised. "We'd barely have time to catch our breath," she says. "You disengage and then head right on stage. I liked to live on the edge. But I think everyone in Cirque lived that way."

She says she looks back on it all and thinks there was a certain kind of honesty to the entire scene. "It's like we were all saying 'we fuck, we get stoned, we party all night, and we don't give a damn.' Life is about experience. If you were anywhere near Cirque du Soleil back then, you probably experienced more extreme living there than anywhere else in the world." Annie says that's why she stayed with Cirque for so many years; she would have had no clue what else to do with her life. Annie says that all the rumours about Laliberté are true, and then some. Yet one of her biggest memories is the time she had a three hour talk with Laliberté, when she found out he did indeed have a compassionate side.

"A friend of his was very sick, and Guy was upset," she remembers. "We sat in a restaurant for hours talking about life. He confided to me that he really doesn't take himself too seriously and that he considers every moment he's alive to be a blessing. From then on I always looked at him in a different way. I realized that he was just another person like the rest of us.

"He told me his dream was to spread positivity to people everywhere and to give them an escape from the grind of everyday life. That was his main reason, initially, for getting involved in busking and then the circus."

8 Cirque was still far from the most successful circus in the world, and so Laliberté prepared for the immense challenge of conquering New York City. He closely monitored the success of Paul Binder and Michael Christensen's traditional Big Apple Circus and decided to make a move to catch them on their home turf.

"It's important not to limit ourselves to just the western part of the U.S.," he said at the time. "To conquer America we need to go east and be successful in the big city: New York." In May 1988, Laliberté would implement one of the greatest plans of his life.

He worked for months in advance to position Cirque properly for its much hyped debut in the Big Apple. Preparation would help him avoid any setbacks. He spent over a quarter of a million dollars in advertising alone, including $75,000 on two full-page ads in *The New York Times*. He plastered the city with posters and flyers and placed advance publicity in all the major media outlets. The venue Laliberté chose was Battery Park—three blocks away from where 9/11 would later occur—within view of the Statue of Liberty.

Cirque sparked more discussion on New York streets that May than the Yankees and Mets put together. As in L.A., there was no shortage of A-listers buying tickets; Mick Jagger, Francis Ford Coppola, Frank Sinatra, and legendary New York mayor Ed Koch all attended. It was the hottest ticket in town.

Opening night sizzled. After their May 25 stage bow, Cirque was embraced by the media in glowing reviews that appeared in *The New York Times*, *The New York Daily News*, and *The New York Post*. Both print and electronic media doled out affection and praise with words like "incredible," "a must-see," and "amazing." Sure enough, Laliberté knew if he could make it there, he could make it anywhere.

"L.A. was the *hors d'oeuvre* and New York was the main course," says New York TV talk-show host Joe Franklin. "Cirque du Soleil's future was sealed once they conquered New York. So many people have come to this city with stars in their eyes and have ended up going home on the next bus without a penny in their pockets. Cirque du Soleil was different. They're an extremely smart organization that knows how to market themselves better than any other group out there. Broadway producers should have been taking notes that summer, because Cirque du Soleil was doing something that few people knew how to do—win over the New York media. It was unbelievable."

New Yorkers not only fell in love with Cirque; they also fell in love with Laliberté. He began to cultivate a unique group of jet-setter friends in New York that he would maintain for life.

"Everyone who was someone in New York wanted to be at the same dinner table, party, or bar as Guy," says former New York club owner, Josh Nichols. "He was charming, likeable, sincere, and highly successful. And he treated everyone with equal respect. I remember one night, he must have been out with thirty people, with bottles of vodka and champagne spread out all over the table. It was amazing to see. Everyone was listening to him speak as if he was the president. You could hear a pin drop; they were grabbing on to his every word. And when he smiled, they all smiled. He had the most infectious way about a person I've ever seen."

Laliberté's soft, mischievous face and matter-of-fact demeanour endeared him to almost everyone he came in contact with. Even though people couldn't always follow his stories because of his thick Quebec accent, he attracted people like flies. They wanted his advice, his opinion, and his approval.

"In a way, he quickly became the king of New York," Nichols says. "He was a complete character. He operated so smoothly. He'd make everyone forget their problems and realize how precious and special life is. The second you meet him you know one thing for sure—Guy loves life. I think until the day he dies he'll live with a smile on his face. I can't say that for too many other people I've met."

Meanwhile, as Cirque became more successful by the minute, its employees were becoming increasingly disgruntled with working conditions. Several had quit the year before in support of Guy Caron. Now, Laliberté was close to losing more talent if things didn't change quickly. Thanks to the sympathetic ear of one of its most influential people, a major walkout was avoided at the last minute. Several performers voiced their concerns to Gilles Ste-Croix and told him how upset they were by the low pay and heavy work days. Ste-Croix, whose politics were fairly socialist, used his persuasive powers to get Laliberté, Gauthier, and Latourelle to agree to review the situation.

"Gilles used street-level judgment," a former Cirque executive says. "He was concerned for the welfare of the performers and crew. He sympathized with the issues they raised and confronted his close friends at the top. He wanted everyone to feel they were being treated fairly, and at this point there was definitely room for big improvements. It was at this time that Gilles added another job to his Cirque resumé: director of human resources."

Ste-Croix had a lot of stamina and worked hard to make things better. Finally, he was able to initiate improvements. Everyone's salary was increased by twenty-five percent and there was no more obligation to do nine shows per week, which was one more than the eight shows per week for top Broadway productions. Instead of paying the performers a weekly salary, they were now to be paid by the performance, between $90 and $115 per show.

Among Cirque's cast and crew, the results were very favourable. The functioning of the entire production improved overall, as everyone now seemed more at ease. Ste-Croix had extinguished a potentially costly fire.

"He was the only one who would be able to talk sense into Guy," a former Cirque executive says. "Gilles was for the people. That's why he busked on the street all those years. I think if anyone else had approached Guy, change would not have gone down as fast. Guy respected Gilles and took seriously whatever he proposed. No fool could ever alter Guy's world no matter how hard they tried, but Gilles had a knack for being able to change Guy's mind. Guy realized the value of Gilles's contribution to Cirque du Soleil and made a big effort to never take it for granted. The last thing he wanted was for Gilles to leave the way Guy Caron did."

The huge success Cirque was enjoying in the U.S. was not enough to cool the emotions in its head offices. A major conflict erupted once again, now between Normand Latourelle and Laliberté. Latourelle tried to mobilize support to oust Laliberté. They had a huge difference in vision and their relationship now was completely dysfunctional. Gilles Ste-Croix told journalist Jean Beaunoyer that it was during a tour in Scandinavia that he received a letter from Latourelle, with instructions to give it to Laliberté. It stated that Latourelle wanted to buy Laliberté's shares in Cirque.

A former Cirque executive says that Latourelle had been conniving behind Laliberté's back to take control. Latourelle had recently separated from his wife, with whom he had two kids, and was having an affair with Laliberté's personal secretary, Nancy Vanasse, from whom he attempted to extract many of Laliberté's secrets.

The feud between the two went on for months before it came to a head, when Laliberté delivered an ultimatum to his partner Daniel Gauthier. He didn't mince words: "It's either him or me." For the next three days, Laliberté didn't show up to work. Technically, this elevated Latourelle into the position of Cirque president. Gauthier realized this was a grave situation; one of these obstinate men had to go.

"This was very serious," says the former executive. "There was no way these two big egos would be able to work together again. By this time they hated one another. It was the most unambivalent relationship I ever saw between two people in Cirque du Soleil."

Gauthier ended the drama quickly; he was not impressed by Latourelle's manoeuvres to oust Laliberté. He became convinced that Latourelle's intentions were not noble and could end up destroying Cirque. Most of all, he feared that down the road Latourelle could attempt the same type of hostile takeover on him. Without Laliberté, Cirque's future would be greatly jeopardized.

"Without Guy Laliberté in Cirque, it would be like Kentucky Fried

Chicken without Colonel Sanders," the former executive explains. "Laliberté was the person everyone associated with Cirque du Soleil. It would have been a major blow to oust him. I don't think Cirque could have lasted, especially since Laliberté was in negotiations with top people in Las Vegas at that time to create permanent shows there. Could you imagine if Guy would have left? The Cirque's biggest cash cow of all time, Vegas, would have never happened. Gauthier was a smart man and realized what would happen down the line. It didn't take him long to make the decision to tell Latourelle to take a hike."

Gauthier called the two men into the same room to deliver his verdict. Laliberté and Latourelle didn't exchange a word and didn't look at each other. The tension between them could be cut with a knife. Gauthier said he wanted to end the possibility of any further hostile takeovers by Latourelle. He told him the end of the line had come and offered Latourelle a buyout package, which he had no choice but to accept.

Latourelle's buyout was nowhere near the rumoured seven figures his friends were led to believe. In fact it was $75,000, with another $200,000 for the ticket selling enterprise called Admission, which he had founded with Gauthier. Admission had quickly become Quebec's version of Ticketmaster, a highly successful company in the U.S. that sold tickets to concerts, sporting, and show type events.

It was at this time that Laliberté became obsessed with studying other successful businessmen so he could learn from their hardships. He read books and watched films on everyone from Howard Hughes and Abraham Lincoln to Vincent van Gogh. He learned from their successes and failures and saw method in their madness. Most of all, he spent tedious hours learning how they dealt with moments of tension and severe conflict.

"Guy pored over document after document about how some of the world's most successful people operated," a close friend of Laliberté says. "He wanted to educate himself by studying a combination of business and art. When he sat down with the powerful people in the world, he wanted to prove that he was knowledgeable and well read. This worked to his advantage, and it was common to see famous rock stars, business moguls, and politicians sitting with Guy at dinners, listening attentively to every word that came out of his mouth. His knowledge was astonishing. He was able to hold his own on any subject, whether it was art, entertainment, cuisine, fine wine, or sports. People who met him were mesmerized by the way he handled himself."

Even if the people at Cirque talked about the Laliberté-Latourelle conflict for months before being able to move on with their lives, Laliberté had a new sense of self-worth. The incident had made him aware of the worst that could happen to him at the hands of "useless" people. He promised Gauthier his decision would pay great dividends.

"This was a turning point," the former Cirque executive says. "Laliberté felt more secure and more determined than ever to make Cirque a huge international success. He had jumped over the biggest hurdle of his life. Now, he resolved to work harder than ever to make Cirque the power house he had so long dreamed of."

9 Laliberté had his dark moods, rages, and silences, but when it came to his friends, for the most part he'd give them the shirt off his back. There were many who found the complex nature of his character fascinating and who were perfectly prepared to pay the price of being his friend.

"Everyone was taken by Guy; as the years progressed, people wanted to be around him more and more," says "Carl," a former friend of Laliberté's. "No matter how much money he made, he still wanted to enjoy the company of all his close friends. He took them to fancy dinners and on trips around the world and tried to let some of his success rub off on them. As long as his friends listened to him, Guy was willing to talk and be in their company. Often he'd spend all night up with them talking, drinking, and having fun and then go into Cirque the next day without having had any sleep. No one knew how he was able to function, but he seemed to never lose a beat."

Now that so many saw him as a man of destiny, Laliberté felt ever more equal to the task of pitting himself against life and limits. After all, he was virtually a prophet in his thriving international business, with a following of Cirque loyalists who were most willing to be led to the promised land. He was Cirque's iconoclast.

An informant close to Cirque, "Denis," says that finally everyone in Cirque began to understand what Laliberté was all about. "In a matter of one year he was able to grab hold of Cirque again, like never before, and start what would be a major conquest of the world; this was never before seen in an arts company from Quebec or Canada. Laliberté was on his way to making Cirque du Soleil one of the world's biggest entertainment commodities in history."

For Laliberté, this was enjoyable and challenging. Never before had anyone seen him work so hard and so passionately. He put all the exasperation and internal politics at Cirque behind him and focused on the job at hand—taking Cirque to a level no one thought possible.

The North American tour of *Nouvelle Experience* was Cirque's most successful to date. Almost 1.5 million people attended the show in Cirque's new 2,500 seat tent. The production was highly acclaimed and received New York's prestigious 1990-1991 Drama Desk Award for most unique theatrical experience. From here on in, there would be no holding back.

Laliberté wanted to maximize revenue streams and dreamed of running multiple shows simultaneously. He hired another *Nouvelle Experience* cast and now had one for North America and another for Europe. This was neither the first nor last time Laliberté took a risk that everyone else doubted.

"What makes guy so special is the way he has continued to silence his naysayers over the years," says Denis. "He went against the grain many times, to the dismay of others. What is so remarkable is the way he was able to make believers out of them in the end. I don't think there's anyone else in the history of Canada who took the giant risks in business, on an international level, the way Guy did."

By the end of 1991, Cirque was dazzling the world with *Nouvelle Experience*. Key showbiz bosses were making inquiries, and Laliberté could now see the possibility of realizing his ultimate dream. He would make Cirque a permanent fixture on Las Vegas's bustling hotel strip, something never before seen. He wanted Cirque to be bigger than any of the famed Vegas acts. It was no small competition: the biggest Vegas act to date was back in the 1960s and was none other than Frank Sinatra's notorious Rat Pack, featuring Sammy Davis Jr, Dean Martin, Peter Lawford, Joey Bishop, and Sinatra himself. But Laliberté was determined to make his mark in Sin City.

"Guy was obsessed with the history of Vegas. He knew if he could get Cirque up and running there it would be a success, because there had never been anything like it before," a former Cirque executive says. "He loved everything about Vegas, from the hot weather to the casinos to the atmosphere on the Strip. He knew that everyone who came to Vegas came for only one thing: to spend money. Whether it was in the casinos or at the live shows, people come to Vegas to have a good time and spend exorbitant amounts of cash. Guy smelled success there. If the right person would give him an opportunity to put Cirque in Vegas, he had no doubt it would turn into gold."

Laliberté was increasingly confident dealing in English, and it wasn't difficult for him to set up meetings. He had some swagger; everything would be done on his terms.

"He was still the same old Guy when he was surrounded by his friends," explains Denis. "But when he went into a business meeting he made sure his conditions were clear. He would not sway at all. By now he realized how important it was to be properly focused. Many people did not like his style, but there were others who shook in their boots when he talked. It's hard to describe, but whatever it was, it was very effective."

Moguls in Vegas were eager to meet with the new, confident Quebec kid in town. Laliberté became flavour of the day. Yet an incident with one of the head honchos at Caesars Palace made Laliberté so angry, he would repeat the story for years to remind people that becoming successful in Vegas was no cakewalk.

The president and CEO of Caesars World, Inc., J. Terrence Lanni, outright refused Laliberté's proposal to present the Cirque's new show, *Mystère*, at Caesars Palace. Laliberté tried to persuade Lanni, but the CEO's mind seemed elsewhere; he listened with an opaque look. Lanni had decided Cirque was not a match for Caesars; it was too dark and esoteric. This enraged Laliberté, who vowed to make Lanni regret his decision.

Laliberté had the ability to argue, assert, and persuade. He was lucid and had an astonishing mind. He was precise, intelligent, and to the point. Most of the time these qualities brought him success.

"It was Guy's dream to bring Cirque to Caesars," says Denis. "He was humbled when his proposal was rejected. Lanni shut the door in his face. Guy never likes to settle for second best, and he became more determined than ever to find Cirque the right home in Vegas. He wanted to make Lanni eat his words."

Laliberté was in a great mood to explore other possibilities in Vegas. Too sure of himself to be detoured by a naysayer like Lanni, he arranged a meeting with another Vegas premium player. Business tycoon and hotel casino developer Steve Wynn had become a key part of Las Vegas history after he raised $630 million to build the Mirage, which features an indoor forest, outdoor volcano, and top quality rooms and service.

Wynn had used Michael Milken-backed junk bonds to open his hotel casino; he was a gambler in almost every move he made. The Mirage, considered a high risk venture when it opened in 1989, became a big hit for tourists visiting Vegas. Its first year occupancy rate was the highest on the Vegas Strip.

Laliberté hit the jackpot with Wynn. Their first meeting was one of perfect timing. Wynn needed to book a show to launch his next project, the Treasure Island Hotel and Casino. The new complex would open right beside the Mirage the following year, in 1993, at a cost of $450 million. Wynn and Robert H. Baldwin, president and CEO of the Mirage, were looking for something dynamic, unique, and lively that could generate a huge buzz on the Strip. Laliberté told them they did not need to look further; Cirque was their answer.

Wynn, who suffers from retinitis pigmentosa, an eye condition that affects peripheral vision, loved the possibility of having Cirque's exotic and family friendly show run full time at his casino. He had been feeling worn down by overseeing the opening of Treasure Island and enjoyed rubbing shoulders with Laliberté. It was stimulating.

"Steve was carrying so much on his plate that he started seeming tired and about to run out of steam, especially to those who knew him," says Andrew Connors, a former business associate. "When Cirque du Soleil came on the scene, it was a much needed breath of fresh air for him. Instantly, he took a liking to Guy Laliberté. Steve was so impressed by Guy's confidence and friendliness. He was much more real and polite than the usual Vegas business sharks Steve had to deal with day in and day out. Guy revived him, making Steve more determined than ever to succeed with a show by his side that many considered a great risk. Steve has always like to play outside the box.

THOMPSON-NICOLA REGIONAL DISTRICT LIBRARY SYSTEM

With Cirque, he went more outside the box than anyone had ever gone before in Vegas. It was very exciting."

Permanence in Vegas excited Laliberté. Back in Montreal, he had been feeling too many forces pressing against him, most notably the bitter Montreal winters. Laliberté has always maintained that he functions best in hot weather, under the *soleil* for which he had named his business. Although his life revolved around the sun, and despite some desire to cut his umbilical cord with Montreal, he still kept a residence in his home city and travelled back and forth.

"Guy is a die-hard Quebecer," journalist Esmond Choueke says. "No matter how much he complained about it, he still loved it. It was a love-hate relationship, with the love being predominant. Sure, he was happy to be in the hot Vegas sun, but as time went on it would wear off. His heart always remained in Montreal."

For now, however, all Laliberté dreamed of was Vegas. He loved the Strip, and often scuttled from one hotel to another until the wee hours of the morning. He fell in love with the unconventionality of Vegas. The bright lights, round the clock entertainment, stampedes of curiosity seekers, and endless opportunities to make cash made Laliberté like a kid in a candy store.

Wynn signed Laliberté and Cirque to a ten-year service contract. Naturally, there were certain escape clauses in case Cirque turned out to be a flop. But negotiations between Wynn and Laliberté were smoother than people imagined they would be, especially those who knew each of the obstinate pair personally.

"You'd think those negotiations would have been extremely hard, considering the two characters involved," says Denis. "But they ended up doing much better than people expected. Guy is stubborn, but only when the person he's dealing with is sort of inferior to him. When he negotiated with people who were more powerful, he'd always be like a mouse. Wynn was one of the biggest players ever in Vegas; it was a cakewalk for him when he initially dealt with Guy. Naturally, that would all change later on down the road. For Guy, dealing with people has always been like a game of cards, and back then Wynn was holding the better hand."

To this day, many credit Wynn as being the visionary who saved Vegas. The city had a history of flirtation with bankruptcy dating back to 1905, when the railroad incorporated the town, and before 1931, when State Assemblyman Phil Tobin was able to convince council to push through the wide-open gambling act. No matter how much success Vegas enjoyed, it had always been plagued by undesirable mobsters and rumours of impending financial ruin.

But the people running Vegas today are far different than the characters who dominated it years ago. Their vibe is more that of Harvard business graduates than gambling, fast living gangsters.

"I don't think Guy falls under either of those descriptions," says Denis. "He was his own person and meant no harm to anyone. He just wanted to live life to its fullest, which he did every second he was in Vegas. As for the undesirables, Guy is no fool. If he realized someone shady wanted to get close to him, he'd make sure they weren't allowed anywhere near. He was well aware of how many undesirables paraded around Vegas. He was in no hurry to hang out with any of them."

Steve Wynn had the great advantage of having learned the art of gambling from his father, who ran bingo halls in upstate New York. Later on Wynn had distributed meat to Vegas casinos and saved every penny he had to invest in the Golden Nugget casino. He hit pay dirt on a land flip, selling a small piece of land he owned to Caesars for its long-planned expansion.

"In 1987 and 1988 people were writing Las Vegas off," Rob Goldstein, president of the Venetian hotel casino tells United Press

International reporter, Joe Bob Briggs. "There had been no new casinos built since the '70s. Places that looked like the Riviera and the Sahara—that was the Strip. There were no new hotels. The last one was MGM, now Bally's, in 1972. The town had stopped. Wynn was clearly the guy who bet the money. Then Kirk Kerkorian came along. Those two guys spawned the Mirage, Excalibur, New York-New York, MGM Grand Las Vegas, Luxor, Venetian, Treasure Island. Suddenly there were tens of thousands of jobs."

Like Laliberté, Wynn was a control freak. The only difference between the two was that Wynn was litigious. If a journalist printed so much as one word he disagreed with, Wynn got his lawyers to sue without any questions asked. "I've been sued by Steve five times," John L. Smith, the respected columnist for the *Las Vegas Review Journal*, told Briggs. "And I'd rather not make it six."

Briggs says it took repeated requests to get Smith to finally meet for breakfast to talk about Wynn. The journalist was wary of how Wynn would react if Smith talked about the litigation surrounding his unauthorized Wynn biography, *Running Scared: The Life and Treacherous Times of Las Vegas Casino King Steve Wynn*.

Wynn's penchant for suing was not only against journalists. His legal battles with the famous real-estate developer Donald Trump are legendary. Each party accused the other of unscrupulous and often unlawful tactics, including spying and wiretapping. Wynn was notorious for siccing private investigators on anyone who tried to stand in his way. Coincidentally, Laliberté had long been fascinated with Trump and had closely monitored how he built and maintained his empire. But business was business, and Laliberté had no real interest in any legal battles his new boss Wynn might engage in with Trump.

Many nights during his early days in Vegas, Laliberté stayed up drinking, gambling, and partying until seven in the morning. He'd stumble in two hours late for meetings with Steve Wynn and the crew developing Cirque in Vegas, but he always seemed alert no matter how late he stayed up.

Laliberté found he could joke and giggle with Wynn almost as if they were lifelong friends. Wynn found Laliberté's laughter warm and cheering. His humour was never cruel or off limits; it was usually directed at himself and based on a sense of the ridiculous. When it came time to work, however, all clowning stopped. Never before had anyone seen Laliberté so serious regarding his work. He carved a reputation for himself as a consummate professional and was always willing to work as long as necessary without complaining. He never drank at work and never held things up. Wynn was impressed by his dedication and brilliance.

Hanging out with Wynn and his cronies was a mentorship experience for Laliberté. He was drawing from the best business role model he would ever have. Before Mystère opened, Wynn made Laliberté go to see all the hit Vegas shows and take notes. Although Laliberté often felt isolated from all his close friends in Montreal, the learning experience was invaluable.

"Wynn gave Guy a new lease on life," says Denis. "Guy had accomplished so much and seemed to be stagnating a bit in Montreal. After the Vegas deal was signed, I had never seen him with so much energy and passion. He was like a kid who had just got accepted to Oxford or Stanford. He recaptured an incredible fresh energy that had escaped him for a while because of all the ups and downs Cirque had gone through over the past couple of years."

Weeks before *Mystère* was scheduled to open, Wynn start to get cold feet. He thought the show was too risqué and told Laliberté he was having second thoughts. He was impressed with parts of the show's cleverness and creativity, but thought overall it was too dark and too racy. He was nervous about how radical a departure it was from the other shows in Vegas, something that had originally appealed to him. He brought Laliberté and Franco Dragone together in his office and gave them a dose of stern reality. After viewing numerous rehearsals, Wynn said that he feared the audience might be put off by the abstract and dark ambience of the piece. He was also worried that media critics might react negatively because it was so different.

He told the nervous pair, "You guys have made a German opera here." Years later Dragone would say he took Wynn's criticism as a compliment. He said the reaction proved how effective the artistic direction of *Mystère* was. Any other reaction, he said, might have made him rethink the show's vision. But behind the scenes, Laliberté took the remarks seriously. Wynn was threatening to postpone the grand opening of the show unless immediate changes were made.

"Guy pretty much flipped out after Wynn threatened to can the show," a former Cirque executive says. "He did everything in his power to turn the situation around quickly. The last thing he wanted was to have to feed the media and public some lame excuse as to why the opening was delayed. He rallied his team to tighten up the entire show. Guy was always a master at moving forward, no matter how bad things got. He can turn any situation around to his benefit. With Wynn it would be more difficult, because he had never been up against anyone so powerful. He was being tested by Wynn and ended up proving his extraordinary capabilities."

The frenetic months leading up to *Mystère* turned into a kind of desperate dance. As the pressure leading up to the grand opening mounted, Laliberté grew to resent the bedlam that he had initially embraced in Vegas. It was as if he were surrounded by buzzing insects; some were nice, some were talented, and some were driving him crazy. But bemoaning his fate was not his style.

"Everyone was tugging away at Guy in the weeks leading up to the opening," Denis says. "He had to keep a distance from most people to concentrate on the enormous task of mounting the show. It took a toll on him, and he started looking worn out, even though he'd never admit it."

The timing of *Mystère* was also the perfect way to launch the tenth anniversary of Cirque. Laliberté told close friends who flew in for the Vegas opening that it was the culmination of a decade of ups and downs.

"For me, it's going to be the biggest night in Cirque's history," he told Denis. "All our hard work will have paid off. I only see this as a positive situation. Even if every critique of the show is negative, I don't think any of us will crawl into a hole and bury ourselves. We've worked so hard to make this happen. We have to hold our heads high, no matter what happens."

Finally, on Christmas Day 1993, Cirque premiered at Treasure Island Hotel and Casino. To Wynn's surprise, the reviews of *Mystère* were spectacular. Dragone's concept wowed both critics and fans, who were treated to an artistic exploration of the origins of life in the universe, combined with a spectacular soundtrack of world beat music rooted in Spanish, African, and Eastern European traditions.

The opening party was the mother of all Vegas parties, one Laliberté will be remembered for forever. No one in Vegas was capable of throwing a more superlative party than Laliberté.

"Guy had everything you could think of for his friends, including the best alcohol, drugs, and hottest women in Vegas," a longtime friend of Laliberté says. "It certainly set the tone for all his future parties, although they seemed to get better and crazier each time. Even if I lived in Alaska and had no money, I'd walk all the way to Vegas to be at his party. There was nothing like it anywhere. People would do anything for Guy, so long as he promised them an invitation to his parties."

For all its excesses, including a whopping seventy-two performers onstage, *Mystère* was a masterpiece production. And permanence in Vegas would mean an opportunity to employ thousands of Quebecers and artists from all over, one can well imagine that not many of Laliberté's recruiting invitations were refused.

*Mystère* runs to this day in Vegas, something Wynn could never have envisioned, even in his wildest dreams. Like Wynn, who had been dubbed a modern-day King Tut, Laliberté was also destined to leave monuments as part of his legacy in the desert. The pair had built the biggest show Vegas had ever seen.

# 10

These were halcyon days for Cirque du Soleil; everything seemed to fall into place. *Mystère*'s success required that Cirque set up permanent offices in Vegas, and although he worked hard, Laliberté lived a life of luxury there. He bought a spectacular penthouse condominium with a jaw dropping view of the desert and was often spotted driving on the Strip in vintage sports cars. He found living in Vegas to be restorative.

"After *Mystère*'s great reviews, Guy had everyone in Vegas at his feet, including Wynn," a former Cirque executive says. "He was now in his early thirties and was living life as if he were king of the world. I once told a friend if I could live one day the way Guy lives, it would be as if I died and went to heaven."

Meanwhile, Laliberté's desert-city deal-making during 1992 and 1993 hadn't impeded other Cirque developments back home. Regular touring Cirque du Soleil shows had been created and mobilized.

Franco Dragone's latest concept, *Saltimbanco*, had been developed for 1992. His inspiration was the multicultural presence at Cirque; he wanted the theme of his newest touring production to be one of "cosmopolitan urbanism." He conceived *Saltimbanco*, the first show in which Cirque presented a complete storyline and a theme that was conceptual from start to finish. Featuring forty-seven artists, the cast had been recruited from more than fifteen countries. *Saltimbanco* would be taken around the world and would become the longest touring show Cirque ever produced.

For Laliberté, *Saltimbanco* stood for something he would try to achieve for the rest of his life—world peace. "For me, Saltimbanco is a message of peace," Laliberté says. "In the 1990s, immigration was an issue—the mixing of cultures in cities—and *Saltimbanco* reflects that mix, with all of its personalities and colours. It's the challenge we have in today's world: respecting each other, living and working together, despite our differences."

After *Saltimbanco* wound up its North American tour, Cirque was invited by the Fuji Television Network to tour Japan in the summer of 1992. They took the best parts of *Nouvelle Experience* and *Cirque Réinventé* to create *Fascination*, the first Cirque show to take place in an arena rather than under their trademark blue and yellow tent. The show was never seen outside Japan.

"Doors just kept opening for Guy," the former executive says. "Things never slowed down; they just kept getting more intense for him. We joked that he seemed to have a horseshoe up his ass. Everything he touched turned to gold."

The creative juices at Cirque kept flowing, and so did the sold out box office receipts. For Cirque's tenth anniversary, more shows were conceived. One night over dinner at a Vegas casino restaurant, Laliberté, Dragone, and Cirque choreographer Juan Isidro Casilla agreed on the concept of a new show which would be dark and extremely provocative.

*Alegria* cost more than $3 million to produce and featured a combination of dark lighting and somber music that was much heavier than past Cirque shows. Dragone says, "I told Guy the next show would be sad, heavy, and really hard." Meaning "joy" in English, *Alegria* toured the world to sold out audiences and its music became Cirque's best selling soundtrack album ever. Laliberté's empire was now estimated to be worth in the hundreds of millions. He received numerous offers to buy Cirque, but refused to take any of them seriously.

"People tried to convince Guy to turn Cirque into Disney, but he wouldn't give in," a close business associate of Laliberté says. "He did everything he could to keep it true to its roots, despite all the money being waved in his face to sell it. He could have easily taken one of the offers, kicked back, and partied and travelled the world for the next ten lifetimes. But he didn't. He was on a mission to keep making Cirque bigger and better, and nothing would stand in his way, not even a billion-dollar offer to take a hike. Cirque probably would have ended up ruined down the line, had he stopped at this point. He wanted to make sure nothing ruined his baby."

More mega-Cirque productions were on the way. *Quidam*, "nameless passerby" in Latin, opened in Montreal in April 1996 as Cirque's ninth production. The show's design team of Franco Dragone and Michel Crête took risks like never before, as they created an overhead rigging system that made it easy for performers to enter and exit from above and across the stage. During the show, cast members could hang in the air for lengthy periods of time by using harnesses.

*Quidam* embarked on a three-year North American tour and played to over 2.5 million people. Not in his wildest dreams did Laliberté— who not so long ago was busking on the streets as a fire-breather—

think he'd be producing shows selling out to millions of people all over the world. Cirque was making history each and every day.

Cirque's incredible successes inspired Laliberté and his partner Daniel Gauthier to build new offices in Montreal. It would be a state of the art environment and would include a world-class training centre. The new Cirque headquarters would be constructed in Saint-Michel, a run down former industrial neighborhood that was next to an enormous garbage dump. No matter how much money Cirque was pulling in, Laliberté wanted to keep Cirque close to its roots, in the street.

Laliberté and Gauthier wanted the new headquarters to facilitate a culture of mutual admiration and understanding between art and business. The entire structure was designed so everyone in the corporate environment of Cirque could look out from large office windows to the dance studios, gymnastics floor, and acrobatic equipment where the performers trained and rehearsed. It was a reminder to everyone that the company was built on the sweat and hard work of its performers.

"Guy wanted to keep everyone grounded by making them remember how things started," Denis says. "He didn't want people to forget where it all came from. He wanted them to show the performers the respect they so well deserved."

The Cirque had a major shakeup after its next show, *La Nouba*. Franco Dragone and Michel Crête decided it was time to move on. Dragone would go on to become artistic director for another legendary Quebec entertainer's show: Céline Dion was going to be opening full time in Las Vegas. Although Dion was by far the most successful solo act ever to emerge from Quebec, her husband and manager René Angélil had long been envious of Laliberté's enormous success. Although just as famous as Cirque in North America and Europe, the Dion enterprise paled in comparison financially. Angélil, a longtime avid gambler, was eager to get a piece of the action and so made an offer to Cirque du Soleil's Dragone that he couldn't refuse.

"Laliberté pretended to support the move, but deep down I don't think he was too impressed by how Angélil yanked his main man," says journalist Esmond Choueke, who has been covering Céline Dion since the beginning of her career. "Their relationship was cordial, but behind the scenes they talked behind each other's back. As supportive as Laliberté was of Dion coming to Vegas, he couldn't have been too thrilled. She'd be competing with him for every tourist's entertainment dollars on the same Strip.

"And let's face it aside from gambling there was nothing else Laliberté had in common with Angélil, who's old enough to be his father. It's not as if they'd be hanging out every night cruising bars and having fun. If Angélil would have tried to keep up with Guy's wild lifestyle for even one night, he probably would have dropped dead of a heart attack on the spot."

For the new show, Laliberté shocked everyone by hiring Guy Caron to replace Dragone. Everyone remembered how years back Caron had unceremoniously walked out on Laliberté and Cirque. Apparently, the two had renewed their friendship in recent years. The new set designer was Stéphane Roy, who had worked with Laliberté and Gauthier years ago at Le Balcon Vert in Baie-Saint-Paul. The people around Cirque were not pleased, as Caron swayed away from Dragone's cutting-edge style and reverted to the more traditional themes of *Cirque Réinventé.*

"Guy always liked to keep an inner circle, even if he sometimes got burned by them," Denis says. "He believed in making happy the people who were with him from the beginning. It's how he was most comfortable operating, even if the current people at Cirque disagreed. I think the way he stayed loyal was one of his best qualities."

With his accumulation of successes, several publishers approached

Laliberté to write his memoirs. He thought it was too early; he told one publisher that until he led a full life with kids and grandkids, he wouldn't be ready to tell his story.

Laliberté would be brought a step closer to this full life when he met the woman who would change his life dramatically. Laliberté was a real ladies' man, yet despite the fifteen-year gap in their ages, he had never before felt the chemistry he had with this new and mysterious woman.

# Part II

# 11

Summer 2006. Montreal is letting loose after the long, hard winter. The stereo in the half-million-dollar sports coupe is blasting loud enough to be heard three blocks away. A tall, marvelously sculpted South American woman is having a ball as she cruises around in the Porsche GT that belongs to her ex-boyfriend, business tycoon Herbert Black. There's much to flaunt; there are only a handful of GTs in Quebec.

When the cops pull over Rizia Moreira to check out the ownership of the vehicle, one of them says he knows of only one other GT on the road in Montreal, and it belongs to a notorious billionaire. "He's my ex," Moreira replies.

\* \* \*

I was introduced to Moreira four years before this summer scene. Our introduction came about after a phone call to my Montreal apartment from Dione Cunha, another olive-skinned, vibrant, and slightly outrageous Brazilian woman. She had recently moved to Montreal to marry my close friend, the president of the La Senza lingerie company, Joel Teitelbaum.

"Ian darling, I need a big favour from you," Cunha said. "I have a friend who needs a lawyer badly. I know your uncle is a well-known judge, and maybe you can ask him a favour."

I told her she was out of her mind. My uncle is Supreme Court Justice Morris Fish, and I could never ask him this kind of favour; I would never use him like that.

As a long-time investigative journalist, one of the first things I had done when I entered the business was surround myself with the best legal counsel - just in case. I had access to several of the top lawyers in the city. I contacted one of them and he agreed to meet her.

I found it strange that Cunha was arranging a meeting for someone who was going against Laliberté. Ever since I first met her eighteen months earlier, she had talked endlessly about how wonderful and magnificent Laliberté was. She repeated numerous times how keen she was to meet him. I guessed she was perhaps eager to make a quick social climb in her new city, or maybe she wanted to meet Laliberté for the drugs. Cunha was a heavy pot smoker and casual cocaine user when I first met her. Either way, hanging out with Laliberté would be the perfect entrée for her into Montreal's elite party scene. "I'd love to get invited to his party," she once told me. "Halperin, do you know anyone who can get us in? I'd do anything to go."

I was also a bit uncomfortable, because like Moreira, Cunha was a large and voluptuous Brazilian dish who came to Canada because she fell in love with a short, balding man who had deep pockets. Both coveted similar men. Was it just a strange coincidence?

The next day I headed over to Moreira's sprawling Montreal

apartment in the luxurious Le Cartier building on Peel Street. I had visited the building many times in the past because my lawyer, Julius Grey, had his office there. A tall young woman wearing sunglasses opened the door. She was wearing an expensive leather coat over jeans. She introduced herself to me as Rizia, and we clicked right away. We went down the street for coffee, chatting nonstop about the beauty of Brazil and of our children. Although she didn't look a day over twenty, she was twenty-seven at the time and had three kids, all with her ex-lover Guy Laliberté.

She went on about the isolation she felt in her adopted city of Montreal, where she spoke a foreign language and had few true friends. I liked her, and I bought into most of what she was saying.

She told me her friend Dione Cunha had mentioned my high-powered uncle, the Supreme Court of Canada judge. She asked if I could call him to get his advice about her plight. I told her it would be most unlikely, but that I did have in mind a lawyer who might be interested. First, I'd need to know all the details, so for the next three hours she dished out all the juicy details.

She told me about the progression of her relationship with Laliberté. Laliberté had been searching for the right woman, one who would neutralize his reputation as a womanizer. But choosing Moreira had turned out to be far from the right formula for that.

It sounded like the most oddball relationship Laliberté ever had. His most serious relationship before that had been with Hélène Dufresne, the stunning Quebec woman he had fallen in love with back in the early days in Baie-Saint-Paul. Their relationship lasted until 1986, when Dufresne realized she could no longer tolerate Laliberté's fast-paced lifestyle. Interestingly, Dufresne would later fall in love with Laliberté's business partner Daniel Gauthier, whom she married in 1991.

Laliberté had met Moreira in early 1992 when he was on what

would become an annual Christmas trip to Brazil. He was smitten by the exotic beauty of the country's landscapes and its people, especially by its gorgeous bikini-clad women. He couldn't stop himself from drooling over the hot babes who paraded semi-nude on Brazil's vast beaches.

One afternoon, while strolling the beach, Laliberté noticed a stunning, tanned model-type girl lying in the sand, soaking up some rays. Never bashful, Laliberté approached her and asked for her name. She barely understood a word, she told me, and motioned to him to leave her alone. But he wouldn't. He tried speaking Spanish to her. He wouldn't leave until she agreed to go out with him.

"At first I wasn't attracted to him at all," Moreira said. "But he was very persistent. In the end, I found him to be quite funny. So despite our huge age difference, I went out with him. We fell in love pretty quickly."

Moreira is from Brazil's rich agricultural and mining region of Minas Gerais. Its capital, Belo Horizonte, has a population of over six million people and its name means "beautiful horizon" in Portuguese. Belo Horizonte has a thriving arts and culture scene and is home to some of Brazil's leading music and dance groups, including Grupo Corpo, the most renowned contemporary dance troupe in Brazil.

Moreira's working-class family instilled in her some strong family values, yet she was the black sheep of her family. Both her sisters ended up living abroad with men who were extremely family-oriented professionals, and one of her brothers would work for Cirque du Soleil for years. She was far more rebellious than the rest of her siblings.

"Rizia always did whatever she wanted and was always the first person to line up for the next big party," says a longtime friend who grew up with her. "But no matter how wild she was, she did have certain characteristics that were commendable. She respected others and she realized the importance of family. That's why, I'm sure, Guy fell in love with her. She came from a solid family and Guy basically wanted someone like that to raise his kids. At the time, he had been unsuccessful in finding the right woman to assume that role. When he met Rizia he thought he had finally met the woman he had been searching for his whole life."

Their unlikely relationship would last ten years and end acrimoniously. It also got off to a contentious start. Moreira's parents vehemently disapproved. They were concerned by the fifteen-year age gap and the long distance aspect of the relationship; they questioned Laliberté's motives.

One evening in particular, Laliberté provoked her father so much that Mr Moreira threatened to call the police. Laliberté had brought along as translator a close friend who was the son of a government minister. In Portuguese, the friend tried to convince Mr Moreira that the five-feet-seven-inch-tall, balding tourist from Quebec was in love with their waiflike daughter, who looked even younger than her seventeen years.

"I don't see a point to this," Mr Moreira replied. "I'm not even sure if it's legal. In some countries this man could go to jail for dating a woman so young. I prefer that they be just friends."

When Laliberté told the Moreiras he intended to bring their daughter to Montreal to see a Cirque show, they hit the ceiling. There was a major hiccup in his plan: the girl could not leave the country without her parents' permission. They had agreed to be guarantors on her passport but told her under no circumstance to leave Brazil. Against her parents' wishes, she convinced a police officer to sign her travel documents and hopped on the next plane to Montreal.

Her parents were far from amused. She remembers her father saying, "I have the obligation to feed and house you, but you can now forget about all those nice things you love so much." When she repeated her father's concerns to Laliberté, Moreira told me all those years later, he answered angrily, "Tell your father to go screw himself." From then on, Laliberté assumed the role of provider so she would no longer have to rely on her parents. He showered her with the best life has to offer, including trips around the world, expensive clothes, and jewelry. Her life was changed forever.

Moreira was ebulliently grateful for the time Guy showed her in Montreal. The couple partied every night, ate at the city's fanciest restaurants, and went on shopping sprees at Montreal's fanciest clothing boutiques.

"Guy showed me the time of my life during my first trip to Montreal," Moreira remembered. "He treated me like a queen, and I felt as if I had met a prince. Looking back, I was so young and naïve; I must have been out of my mind thinking that."

Nonetheless, she became reliant on Laliberté, to whom she looked for learning and protection, and he became her guide. She hoped he would tame her of the wild ways of her past. Little did she know that his own wildness would ignite, rather than extinguish hers. With such earnest expectations, Moreira was setting herself up to be betrayed.

"She was taken in to become Guy's prize possession," a close friend of the ex-couple says. "And she was more than willing to play the part. Guy needed a gorgeous supermodel-like woman to be at his side wherever he went. It was good for his image and great for his business. What Rizia didn't realize was that one day it might all end. Although Guy might be one of the nicest people one could ever meet, he was a jet-set party animal whose wealth and power were extremely attractive to some of the world's most beautiful women. There was no way his relationship with Rizia would last. It was as predictable as snow in

ZUMA
Keystone Press

**Cirque du Soleil in Sao Paulo, Brazil**
February 6th, 2008; Sao Paulo, Brazil

# Guy Laliberté

Ian Halperin

**One of the rare photos of Rizia and Guy when they were together**

Keystone Press

**Guy Laliberté and Claudia Barilla at the world premiere of Cirque du Soleil's Wintuk at Madison Square Garden**
November 8th, 2007; New York City, NY, USA

Retna
Keystone Press

**Guy Laliberté at Gotham Hall in New York City at the Never Follow Bash hosted by Audi & Conde Nast to honour outstanding individuals**
Jun 9th, 2003; New York City, NY, USA

# Guy Laliberté

Michel Ponomareff/
Ponopresse/International / Gam-
ma/Eyedea Presse

**Guy Laliberté and Jacques Villeneuve in the Paddock at the
Montreal Grand Prix**
June 7th, 2008; Montreal, Quebec, Canada

Sutton Motorsports/ZUMA
Keystone Press

**David Coulthard, a driver affiliated with Red Bull Racing, on
the grid with Guy Laliberté in Monte-Carlo, Monaco at the
2007 Formula One World Championship.**
May 27th, 2007; Monte-Carlo, Monaco

Geneviève Larivière
Keystone Press

**Le Cirque du Soleil practice its Kooza show at Les Galeries de la Capitale in Quebec City, Canada**
July 4th, 2007; Quebec City, Quebec, Canada

Big Pictures UK
Keystone Press

**Another artist of the Alegria show by Cirque du Soleil at Royal Albert Hall in London, UK**
January 3rd, 2007; London, UK

# Guy Laliberté

Ian Halperin

**Rizia with the Sony Mini DV Camera that she used to film Guy at his house in bed with two women.**

Ian Halperin

**Ex Brazilian fashion model Dione.  She was the person who introduced Ian to Rizia.**

# *The Fabulous Life of the Creator of Cirque du Soleil*

Barry Sweet/ZUMA
Keystone Press

**Larry King, Paul McCartney, Yoko Ono, Olivia Harrison, Ringo Starr and Guy Laliberté (far right) at the Las Vegas premiere of The Beatles 'Love' by Cirque du Soleil**
Jun 26th, 2007; Las Vegas, Nevada, USA

WENN.com
Keystone Press

**Guy Laliberté, Ringo Starr and his wife Barbara Bach celebrating the legacy of 'The Beatles' at The Mirage in Las Vegas**
June 30th, 2006; Las Vegas, Nevada, USA

# Guy Laliberté

Francois Turgeon
Area 53

**Domain of Guy Laliberté, in the suburb of Montreal, where he organizes his legendaries fiestas for the jet set of the World.**

Francois Turgeon
Area 53

**An architecture which combines the ancient and the modern, in the manner that Cirque du Soleil renews a genre dating back to Antique**

# Guy Laliberté

Michel Ponomareff/
Ponopresse/International / Gam-
ma/Eyedea Presse

**Guy Laliberté gives a press conference for Cirque du Soleil's
25th birthday**
February 8th, 2009; Montreal, Quebec, Canada

Montreal in January."

For Laliberté, there was a sense of recognition and inevitability. It was satisfying to his ego to have such a stunning, worldly woman by his side. It was a glorious affirmation of his manhood. He loved the way she looked and dressed and stood beside him with such instinctive grace. The love affaire reshaped both of their lives.

Moreira said she had a hard time overcoming her isolation from Laliberté's peers, even during her first trip to Montreal. His friends may have been put off by her neediness; nor did they like having to compete for his attention.

"A lot of his close friends were nice to my face, but behind my back they were talking," Moreira said. "They were jealous of how much time he spent with me. I was taking up time that he could have spent with them or working on Cirque. I sensed quite a bit of resentment early on, but I never tried to focus on the negative. I wanted things to be good, so I ignored the bad."

For the next two years, the lovebirds travelled all over the world, stayed in the finest hotels, and lived *la vida loca*. They both shared a passion for travel, romance, and sex. Often the pair would make love five times a day.

"I love sex," Moreira once told me. "In Brazil, it's part of our culture. Everyone is always having fun. It was one of the major reasons why my relationship with Guy was so good in the beginning; we were very passionate about each other. Eventually it changed and split us apart. "

The couple jet-setted to Japan, Spain, France, and L.A., a city Moreira was not particularly fond of. "It's very fake," she said. "I prefer New York. It's more my type of city, because it never sleeps." For her eighteenth birthday they danced all night at a trendy disco in Tahiti. Laliberté went all out and booked the best hotel room on the island

and showered his girlfriend with expensive gifts, including a diamond necklace. He spent money on her like it grew on trees.

"In the beginning of their relationship, the sky was the limit," a close friend of the ex-couple says. "When Guy goes all out, there's not a person in the world who is capable of keeping up with him. He wanted to give Rizia everything under the sun to show her how much he loved her. What he didn't realize was that in the process, he was creating a monster, a woman who started believing she deserved only the best life has to offer. It was the thing Guy would most regret down the road."

During the initial two years of her relationship with Laliberté, Moreira left Brazil to visit him thirteen times. Her parents were concerned she would not graduate from high school because all her attention was being channeled to her rich lover from Quebec.

She told Laliberté she wanted to come to Canada permanently to study architecture. Laliberté promised to finance her studies if she chose Montreal. "Where would I live?" she asked him. "With me," he replied.

Laliberté told her he wanted to have kids but with no strings attached. "He once told me he wanted to have a lot of them, whether with me or other women," she said. "But whenever I brought up marriage, he'd get angry. I realized I was with a man who had no intention of ever walking down the aisle. It broke my heart."

Clearly, as the relationship progressed, Laliberté's mind was not on anything more than being lovers. She was already the main presence in his incredible life, always at his side at fancy galas, openings, and business functions.

When she moved to Montreal in 1995, Moreira's life changed

forever. She enrolled in French language courses at McGill University and worked hard to learn Quebec's culture and language. She worked on the side as a model, enrolling in one of the city's top modelling agencies. The tall, lanky Brazilian was taken for a model wherever she went. She dressed and presented herself as if she had just walked out of a Vogue fashion shoot.

Moreira also got a crash course in Montreal partying. Her name was on the city's top nightclubs VIP lists, and for the first time in her life she started dabbling in drugs. Cocaine was her drug of choice, and she used it occasionally to help her energy levels.

"I was never into drugs before I met Guy," she told me. "I used to party a lot in Brazil, but it never involved drugs, I'd just go out dancing all night with friends. Meeting Guy brought me into a whole new world. He was really into drugs, and I went along with it. How else could I keep up with him? I was so young and naïve back then."

The honeymoon wouldn't last long. Laliberté's heavy Cirque commitments often forced him to be on the road. When she tagged along, Moreira would fall behind in her school work. She had become disoriented by Laliberté's fast-paced life. And there was always the marriage question. It was a struggle between the playboy and the model: she wanted to get married, and he wanted to go to bed.

Viewed today, the battle seems old-fashioned. Yet it's a battle that was clear; there was no ambivalence about commitment. Laliberté didn't want to be domesticated, while Moreira was intent on it. Could one blame her? The man she was with was one of the most powerful and successful ever in Canada. He was notorious for dating strippers, dancers, and models from all over the world. When he was with her he was a perfect gentleman and offered her a glitzy life that most people could never dream of. Her passivity at the beginning of the relationship led her to be swept along in committing her life to him.

As the months passed, it was no surprise to see Laliberté become more of a father figure to Moreira. He seemed to feel some combination of pity and sexual attraction for her, but not true love. And yet she returned love and loyalty to him. In her obsession for love and family, she accepted almost anything Laliberté threw at her.

When she called him on the road, oftentimes other women would answer. "I knew he was seeing other women on the side," she told me. "But what could I do? It would have been wrong for me to accuse him of anything because when I'd go back to Brazil to visit my family, I certainly didn't stay home at night and stare at the four walls."

When she began to feel deserted, she turned to others for the warmth and security that Laliberté was not providing. She started to feel emotionally separated from Laliberté.

"His mood swings were too much for me," she said. "One day he would be nice; the next he would be yelling and screaming at me. I used to cry almost every day. I started to feel so alone."

A close friend of the ex-couple, however, paints a different picture. He says Moreira's constant immature behaviour and insecurities made Laliberté emotionally numb.

"She was never happy, no matter how hard Guy tried," the friend says. "He started to get very tired of it all. If Rizia didn't get her way, she'd lose it emotionally. She couldn't accept the fact that Guy had a busy schedule and a load of commitments that would minimize their time together. She didn't realize that all the expensive clothes and lavish lifestyle she had were paid for by Guy showing up to work. I think she thought money grew on trees. She started to act as if she was queen of

Montreal and everyone should cater to her every whim. No matter how much money Guy made, he never stopped working hard. I don't think this woman ever worked a day in her life.

"Rizia was always trying to make Guy feel guilty. I think she did it because she felt neglected. It wasn't difficult to predict this union wouldn't last long. They were so opposite and yet in some ways so alike, but no matter what, there was no way it was going to last."

Eventually, Laliberté told Moreira he was starting to have doubts about the relationship. She told me she broke down in tears and felt lost and alone. He denied he was seeing other women, but when Laliberté left on a trip to Sardinia, in the Mediterranean Sea, she booked a ticket on the next plane to follow him. She was convinced he was meeting up with another woman on his $35-million sailboat.

She spent two weeks trying to track him down before booking a flight to Berlin, where she knew he would show up at a premiere. At his hotel, she showed up at his door to see if he was alone or with another woman. Laliberté told her she couldn't come in, but through the crack of the door she could see someone else's suitcases. Finally Laliberté let her into the room, where a well known black model was sitting on his bed. Moreira tried to attack the woman, but Laliberté held her back. Desperate, Moreira threatened to jump from the room's large window, telling Laliberté she wanted to create a huge scandal for him. He begged her not to jump.

"He told me to get on with my life and not to do something crazy," she said. "I had never been so upset in my life. I was in love with him, and he was playing me for a complete fool. I wanted to kill myself. Our relationship had become a joke, filled with cheating, violence, and lots of stupid games."

Whether or not there was real violence, only Moreira and Laliberté know. Their pattern resembled that of many violent couples: traditional values, possessiveness, emotional distance, mistrust, anger, and rebellion.

Moreira claimed that several times Laliberté knowingly transmitted sexual diseases to her, to the point where she grew progressively more depressed and worried about her own health.

"He'd come home after sleeping with other women and have sex with me," she told me. "He gave me sexual diseases which could have been avoided if he had been up-front with me. In the beginning I didn't want to believe he was cheating on me, so I looked the other way. If he had told me, I would have never had sex with him. I was furious one morning when I woke up with a rash. Not only was he being unfaithful, he was putting my health at risk." Moreira said that by then she longed to escape from Laliberté, but was feeling too run down and emotionally exhausted.

She also feared for Laliberté's health because he was a chain smoker, a heavy drug user, and a drinker.

"Guy and I both smoked a lot," she said. "It wasn't the healthiest environment. I couldn't quit smoking because I started very young. I ate healthy to try to balance it out, but Guy was completely out of control. He didn't seem to care at all about his health. It was as if he thought nothing could harm him, that he was above life. The way he was going, I thought he would die a very young man and that eventually it would all catch up to him. I guess I was wrong. I have to admit that he's one tough character who can take more than almost anyone else. Not to say it's a good thing, but there was no way he was going to let anything stand in his way in life. Not me, not drugs, nothing. Maybe that's why I fell in love with him, because of how extreme he is."

Moreira began to realize that people were drawn to her connection to Laliberté more than they were to her. She started to resent the social  business that had attracted her in the first place; she started to feel used.

"People used me to get close to Guy," she said. "I really didn't know who to trust. I needed to get a life—my own life. Unless I took action, I'd end up a very unhappy person. I thought about killing myself several times; that's how depressed I became."

Later on that year, Moreira would succeed in becoming more of her own person. But for Laliberté, it was would not be greatest episode in his life.

# 12

As my initial meeting with Moreira wore on, it was increasingly evident that she was furious with Laliberté about everything that had happened. And she was furious with herself for accepting it all so readily and then for feeling guilty about it. She was clearly overcome by anger. She could not hide her confusion and torment and took one shot after another at the man who had brought her a life of luxury, lust, and complete chaos.

She said it was neither the first nor the last time that someone had fallen victim to Laliberté's powerful charm and been so utterly deceived by his unique guise. Moreira looked back on it as the most tormented period of her life.

"It was no wonder he was the master of the circus," she continued that day. "He was a master of deception and tricks and stunts. The problem was that it was at my expense. I put everything I had into Guy, all my love, my life, and my future. I got burned badly. I needed to do something to change my life because I was sinking further by the day.

I realized I made a big mistake by falling for everything he told me. I cannot believe how stupid I was."

Many of the people close to the ex-couple whom I interviewed for this book had mixed feelings about them. A close friend of Moreira blames her increasingly unstable emotions as the main reason the relationship fell apart.

"Guy was a very busy man, and Rizia wanted his attention all the time," the friend says. "He just couldn't keep up with her emotional imbalance anymore. She was up and down like a yo-yo; one second she was happy, and the next she was miserable. No matter what actually went down, I'm not about to throw her any sympathy. Guy gave her everything under the sun, a life of excess that very few are privileged to. How can one feel sorry for her? When you hear Rizia's version of the story, she makes it almost sound as if he tried to kill her. It's the furthest thing from the truth. I was around it all back then, and let me tell you, Guy did everything he could to make her happy. She just wasn't. Happiness starts from within, and she didn't realize that. She thought happiness was the next pair of shoes at Holt Renfrew or the next plane ticket to Dubai."

Moreira's lifestyle began to change after Laliberté tried to convince her to go back to Brazil. She begged him to change his mind. Not long afterward, there was a confrontation in which Laliberté threatened to call the police. Moreira started off by calling him names, and a pushing and shoving match between the two ensued. "Back off, or else I'll call the police," Laliberté said. Then he gave in. "You can stay in my apartment. When I'm here, we'll sleep in separate rooms."

Still, they'd often sleep together. Almost each night they were together, the routine would be similar. They'd start off with a screaming match, and by the end of the night they'd be rubbing their naked bodies together in bed. Moreira was in a phase where sex was her first concern. She told friends she had to have sex every day and that she was constantly thinking about it. After school, while driving home, she was already thinking about having sex that night, even when Laliberté was out of town. Every night that she went clubbing, there was a lineup of men trying to take her home.

"Every time Rizia walked into a room, there was a lot of sexual heat," says a close friend. "Especially when Guy was out of town. It would be hard to find one guy in the room who didn't have his eyes on her. Rumours were going around that her and Guy had split. Who wouldn't have wanted to bed Guy's ex? There was never a woman in the room who came close to exuding the sexuality she did. She'd usually get up on the dance floor and dance alone, which would last no more than five seconds. As soon as she'd start, there would be some guy in front of her trying to become her partner for the night. She attracted men like no other woman I ever saw in Montreal. She was a star."

Laliberté was no slouch himself. In his prime, when he was a fire-breather busking for his next meal, he had a perfectly proportioned body, with long hair and a smile that made women melt. As the years progressed and his partying habits intensified, so did the fat on his body, but he was still was handsome. He sported the pot belly of a man in his mid-thirties who'd spent the past twenty years living a wild bachelor's party life. But he always dazzled with his kind, wise, and charming character. Where Moreira was excitable, Laliberté was a river—calm on the surface, but with powerful currents deep below.

Moreira started spending a great deal of time at a club Guy owned and where an ex-football player worked as a bouncer. She was attracted to him from the moment she first laid eyes on him; some fun would do her a world of good. One night, in the back room of the club, the ex-football player slipped his tongue into Moreira's mouth, and she closed her eyes and enjoyed the moment. A couple of hours later, they went back to Laliberté's apartment and indulged in some heavy moaning and breathing. Laliberté was out of town for a couple of weeks, in Vegas on Cirque business.

A few weeks later, Moreira called Laliberté on the phone, confused and disillusioned. She had just found out she was pregnant. "Maybe it's you who had the infertility problem," she told him.

Despite their breakup, Laliberté remained jealous. He was crushed when he found out Moreira was having an affair with another man. He still spoke of her with affection.

"She was like family to Guy, like a sister or mother figure," says "José," a close friend of Laliberté. "Despite all their arguments and all they'd been through with their nasty breakup, he would not talk bad about her, especially in public. He was still fond of her and wished her the best. On the other hand, he was happy to be single again. Guy likes to get his cake and to eat it too. With Rizia, he had finally met his match. She just didn't put up with it."

Moreira weighed her options. She wondered if raising a child would help heal all the hurt she had inside. She wasn't sure. She was very confused and made one of several suicide attempts in her life. Never before had she been so depressed and lost.

"My dream was always to have lots of children," she told me. "But not in a situation where it was a mistake or wasn't right. I had to make a decision that was very difficult. I hated myself for getting into such an awful situation."

She said her fear about having the baby was that it would grow up without a father; her relationship with the football player had gone sour. She finally made up her mind and booked an appointment at a Montreal abortion clinic. After the procedure, she lay in bed at Guy's apartment recuperating, devastated. She had deep regrets about how things had turned out.

"It was the most difficult thing I ever did," she said. "After the abortion, I didn't know if I was coming or going for a long time. I was drained, both physically and mentally."

Incredibly, the person who consoled her most was none other than Laliberté himself. Although he had given up any notion of possession of Moreira, he continued to be her friend and confidant. His attitude towards her was complex. He seemed to mistrust or disdain what he could possess and worship what he could not. Despite all they had been through, he was there to give her affection when she needed it most.

When she told Laliberté what had happened, he responded in a way she never imagined possible. He was remorseful and broke down in tears and consoled her. The pair spent the rest of the night holding a vigil for the aborted child and cried openly in each other's arms. There was a glimmer of hope for the couple.

"I'm sorry about what's happened," Laliberté told Moreira, holding her in his arms like a baby. "I didn't want things to happen like this." Despite the exhausting prospect of shoring up her unstable identity, he showed he could be incredibly sensitive.

"Guy has more compassion than anyone I've met," José says. "It's just that most of the time he's forced to put up his defenses because everyone is always asking him for favours. It's a very difficult way to live life. But he's the most giving and caring person you'd ever want to meet. He has lived his life helping others make their dreams come true, just like the way he brought Rizia from a life of struggle in Brazil to Canada. I've never heard him ask anyone for anything. The thing about Guy is that he is fulfilled by making others happy; it's a beautiful thing."

Not long after the abortion, Moreira headed back to Brazil to be comforted by her family. She had decided this on her own, but with Laliberté's support. She needed a change of scenery;

in Montreal she had grown more depressed and had once again contemplated suicide. She desperately needed unconditional love and devotion. Anything less at this point was unbearable to her. Her family was her only answer.

"I'm a very lucky person because I always had a great family to fall back on," Moreira said. "No matter what I did, they were always there for me, especially when there was a crisis. Family is the most important thing in life. Without my amazing family, I don't think I would have been able to make it through everything that happened in my first couple of years in Montreal."

By the end of 1995, as she retreated and reached deep within to try and find herself, Moreira and Laliberté had become completely emotionally and physically separate for the first time. But it wouldn't last long.

Moreira missed Laliberté's support and nurturing. They started talking again every day on the phone. They became restless and anxious for each other's company. Laliberté paid her way to meet up with him in the Bahamas at New Year's. When she arrived, she told Laliberté she planned to move to London to pursue her modelling career. She had become obsessed with establishing herself in a career. A top London modelling agency had expressed interest in signing her and told her she had a shot at being the next Naomi Campbell.

Once again, Moreira was stirring things up in Laliberté's world. He begged her to reconsider and practically threw himself at her feet for another chance. He insisted he was finally ready to pay the price of being her boyfriend and agreed to cut out the women and the partying that had so long dominated his errant lifestyle. After much convincing, she agreed to join him in Montreal for Valentine's Day. That night, the first of their three children was conceived.

"No one knows how to get their way better than Guy," Moreira told me. "When he sets his mind to something, he always makes sure it happens. I had decided to start a new life in London, and nothing could stop me from going there except one thing—Guy. I really did not want to go back to Montreal; I wanted to make a fresh start. But he said all the right things to make me change my mind.

"Once again I was back in his life, with him trying to be in command. Nobody was more surprised than I that he was able to convince me of this. Most of my friends and family thought I was nuts. But then again, they thought almost everything I did was crazy. So as surprising as this was, I don't think too many people were shocked."

Their first child, a girl, was born in late 1996. Moreira and Laliberté both figured that with children in the picture, their long history of fighting and abuse would not be difficult to put behind them. Their assumption turned out to be wrong. She demanded that he marry her so their baby girl would be brought up in a proper family setting. He outright refused.

Quebec is singular in North America; its civil code stipulates that a common-law union does not confer the same status or rights as legal marriage. Everywhere else in Canada, common-law couples gain the same rights as married couples after living together for a certain period of time. And while more than a third of Quebec couples are not legally wed, the province's division of assets laws only pertain to those who are. As such, in Quebec, there is no claim to be made on the assets of the other when a common-law relationship ends, regardless of the number of years the individuals were in the relationship together.

"I was completely blind," Moreira said. "There were certainly times when Guy promised to marry me, but he was deceiving me; he really didn't mean it. I turned out to be just another business transaction for him because I had his kids. He once told me he wanted to leave as many kids in the world as possible before he left. He started his mission with me."

Not surprisingly, things didn't work out they way the couple planned. Moreira told me that Laliberté continued his role as provider, but left the task of caring for the baby mostly up to her and a live-in nanny. She said he was a caring father, but he continued to travel more often than he was at home, which left her to battle yet another emotional crisis. Their relationship had once again dissolved.

"Having a baby was supposed to change things," she told me. "Instead it created a bigger gap between us. Guy was always working and travelling and didn't have much time to spend with us. I was very sad, because I thought he would slow down and focus on being a family with us. He was more absent than ever before."

The couple had just moved into a sprawling custom-designed mansion in Saint-Bruno, the quaint town on the outskirts of Montreal where Laliberté grew up. He spared no expense and had each room filled with furniture and art from a different exotic country. There was a large indoor swimming pool, spectacular views, and a full-time kitchen and household staff. The multi-millionaire and his lover were now living in one of the most palatial pads on the planet.

"When we moved in there I was lonely and isolated," Moreira said. "I missed my friends and the action of downtown. In the new house, with just me and a new baby, I felt completely lonely and far away. It was kind of scary."

By mid-1998, rumours spread that Laliberté was worth over a billion dollars. The Cirque du Soleil had kept expanding its presence in Vegas and had several shows touring the world full time. The money was rolling in like never before. But on the home front, things could not have been more unstable.

Laliberté told Moreira he thought they should separate. She broke down and begged him to stay together for the sake of their one-and-a-half-year-old daughter. They decided to go into couples counselling. It was not the outcome she had envisioned.

"Guy is very powerful, and people do whatever he asks," she said. "He pays people to do things. That's what happened in our counselling. He dragged me into it to sign a paper that he could use to keep me from coming back at him and asking for money."

Things for Moreira got much bleaker. Laliberté got her pregnant again. No matter how much arguing went on between them, they always seemed to end up having sex, even if it was sporadic. It was a real love-hate relationship. This time Moreira miscarried, and again, Laliberté was there to console her. She became pregnant again shortly after, but this time, she threatened to leave Laliberté and start a new life elsewhere. She had had enough and wanted to finally break away. Laliberté promised her for the umpteenth time that he'd change. Later that year, her father died, and Laliberté, she claimed, took advantage of her period of grief and convinced her to stay with him.

"He felt terrible that my father died, and he gave me emotional support," Moreira said. "It was a very low point in my life, and I really had no other choice but to stay with him and try to make it work. I had become so dependent on Guy that with one small child and another on the way, it would have been extremely hard for me to start over. So I tried again. It wasn't easy, because deep down I knew what would eventually happen again."

Another dichotomy in the couple's relationship was the difference between their life as a couple at home and their busy public life. "When we were together at home, things were pretty simple, despite living in a very big house," she said. "But the problem was that those nights were too few and far between. Something always seemed to come up that would force Guy to be away."

After the couple's second child, a boy, was born, tensions between them heightened further. Laliberté had been overseas and missed the birth of his son. She accused him of being away partying. He insisted it was for business.

Moreira told me that by 1999, in her mind, the relationship was all but over. She said that Laliberté convinced her to stay together until the end of the year. "Why don't we wait to see if the world ends," Laliberté said jokingly. "If it continues, so should we."

Over the next year, the couple re-established their love and had a third child, another girl, who was born in Brazil. Not long after, Moreira delivered an ultimatum to Laliberté: marry me or it's over. Laliberté at first responded he wanted a permanent split, that he needed a new start, and Moreira didn't fit into his plans. And yet they ended up agreeing once again to stay together for the sake of their three children. But an incident later that summer would be the true and final blow to the couple's ten-year relationship.

Laliberté had close ties to the Formula One circuit and was renowned for his annual Grand Prix party the night of the race in Montreal. He'd long had a fascination with sports cars and was good friends with many of the world's top race car drivers. In the summer of 2001, the German tabloid *Bild* caught Laliberté having sex with a stripper on the yacht of the Formula One race-car driver, David Coulthard.

After this, things erupted between Moreira and Laliberté like never before. She threatened to reveal his intimate secrets to the media and told him she was going to seek full custody of their three children. He promised her he'd fight her to his very last dollar.

"I told him I would reveal everything to the media, so people would know what type of man he really is," Moreira told me. "I was going to say everything about all the money he stashed in his private jet and placed offshore and all the women he's had behind my back. I told him for someone who was the father of three children he was acting without any responsibility. His behavior was unacceptable, but there was nothing I could do. Guy thinks he's larger than life and can do whatever he wants, even if it's at the expense of the people closest to him."

For Moreira, it was the final straw. No matter what, she would never go back to Laliberté. After the devastating episode on Coulthard's yacht, she sat for days and pondered her life while watching her three young children. She wondered how she'd made such a mess of her life.

"It took me a long while to be able to think straight," she said. "I had no job skills, and I had three kids to watch. I would have to start completely over. It was very hard, but I quickly learned a lot. I had two choices: either sit back and fall apart, or pick myself up and do what was right for my children."

For the next few months the couple continued to live together, but they led totally separate lives. They even slept in the same room, in separate beds. Even more complicated than that, Moreira told me, her best friend, whom everyone called Kiwi, was also sleeping in the same bedroom as her and Laliberté. They had a bunk-like contraption rigged up above the bed, and Kiwi would sleep above them. When Laliberté was home, Moreira would climb up top with Kiwi.

"By then we were totally separate," Moreira said. "I agreed to stay in the house for the sake of the kids, but after that incident in the summer I couldn't look Guy in the face anymore. I had lost any respect I had left for him."

Kiwi would become the center of conversation on another occasion, when, the summer following our first meeting, I asked Moreira to help me out at an annual yoga retreat I had founded. The retreat was in Quebec's picturesque Eastern Townships, about ninety minutes outside of Montreal. Moreira had brought Kiwi along.

Nick Chursinoff, a Vancouver musician I knew from the days when I used to earn a living playing saxophone, was also there. At one point during the retreat Nick took me aside and told me, "Ian, you know that woman Kiwi who's with Rizia? She's not a woman. She's a man." At first I thought the fresh country air had gone to Nick's brain or maybe he was tripping on acid and was starting to hallucinate. He told me to look at her Adam's apple and see for myself. After going into the yoga room where Kiwi was warming up, I could not help but notice the bony bump at her throat. She also had a rather deep voice. Nick was not joking. Moreira's friend was a man.

A couple of days after the retreat was over, I confronted Moreira. She admitted Kiwi was a man and explained he had come to Canada from Vietnam as a small boy and decided to get a sex change in his early teens.

"She looks good as a woman, don't you think, Halperin?" she asked me. "A lot of my friends who are men are interested in her; they don't know she's really a man." She told me, "I know one top lawyer in his seventies who was so taken by her that he wined and dined her and made out with her in front of me. If he had known she was a man, I think he would have died on the spot of a heart attack!" I understood. I had actually had my eye on Kiwi since our first meeting because of her striking looks. Needless to say, I was now ready to reconsider.

Several months before that yoga retreat in 2003, Moreira had finally moved out of Laliberté's mansion. The relationship had become unbearable; all the couple did when they were together was argue, even in front of their three children.

"Our relationship had long been over," Moreira told me. "Moving out was only a formality. I needed to get hold of my life. Guy was furious when I left because he realized he couldn't control me any longer. He was worried I'd hook up with a new man who might become a father figure to our children. He had people who would report to him my every move, like the house staff he hired to take care of the kids for me. I'm sure every move I made was being documented. Even though we weren't living together, he still managed to have a lot control in my life."

He feared she might try to take them to live in her native Brazil.

"How could you blame him?" José explains. "Rizia was a loose cannon. She didn't know if she was coming or going. At least Guy could make decisions and make sure the kids were in a stable environment. He had a lot of concerns. He was worried she'd try to hop on a plane with the children and bring them back to Brazil with her. Guy took every precaution he could to make sure the children's welfare was protected.

"Rizia threatened to do everything to him you could think of. She seemed intent on trying to get back at him any way she could; it got very ugly. It was sad for all their friends who cared so much about them. They're great people, but very stubborn. We hoped they would work it out properly for the sake of the children."

They had a colourful host of friends—gays, transvesties, business people, dancers, and drug dealers. Moreira told me that, aside from Kiwi, every friend they had chose to side with Laliberté. She said she learned a life lesson about allegiance.

"They all sided with Guy; they had no choice," she said. "If they didn't, they would never get into all his fancy parties and functions again. I learned who's real and who's fake. To this day, I believe that I would never have been friends with any of those people had I not been Guy's girlfriend. It hurt me a lot, but I got over it. People who dump you like that don't deserve to even have friends."

Close friends believe the whole thing it should have been resolved from the start. The problem was Moreira and Laliberté each wanted to have the final word.

# 13

A few weeks later, back in her apartment at Le Cartier, I took a seat on the sofa in the living room while she checked her mail and phone messages. She offered me a glass of wine and turned on some Brazilian music for me. While I listened to the music, she went to her bedroom and changed clothes. As I got more comfortable, Rizia came out wearing a see-through tank top. She turned off the lights, and started giving me a foot massage.

Did she want to do something sexual? We had never before been intimate, even though we had often slept together in the same bed when we had sleepovers with our children. My daughter is the same age as Moreira's youngest daughter, and every weekend we'd all pile into her Mercedes wagon and, go on outings together. I, too, had recently gone through a split, and, thanks to our mutual friend Dione Cunha, Moreira and her three children were now my surrogate family. We did everything together, and we talked on the phone at least twice a day.

My heart started beating faster. I wasn't sure if it was a ploy or if we were about to have sex. "Relax," she said. "I just need to be touched. We can be open with each other, Halperin." She frequently called me by my last name.

After about half an hour of caressing one another, we went to lie down in her bed. She took off her clothes, and for the first time I got a clear view of her naked body. She caught me looking at her boobs and seemed a bit shy. "Once I settle up with Guy I'll fix them," she said, referring to her breast implants, which seemed to be slightly falling apart. "I need to get them redone. I think I'll get them done in New York; I don't trust anyone in L.A. or Montreal. They charge so much and don't do a good job."

In her large, comfortable bed, Rizia stretched and turned over to face me. She began to confide some personal secrets.

"I'm seeing a guy now, Halperin, but it's nothing serious," she said. She was referring to a guy she had recently met who drove a Porsche around Montreal. He was a well-known Montreal corporate lawyer. "I don't want to be tied down. After Guy, I want to have as much freedom as I can. I've dated several guys since we broke up. I need to have men in my life; I like physical contact."

Then, she asked me why I hadn't made a pass at her. I told her I preferred being friends and that it was a great situation for us, as we were both single parents. It was an amazing opportunity to hang out and feel like a family, even though we weren't a couple.

Moreira turned over to her other side, laughing. "I'm not saying I want to fuck you," she said. "But something is weird here. Usually men just want to fuck me. You're different."

We enjoyed many "family" excursions together. One time we took the kids snow tubing in Saint-Sauveur, fifty minutes north of Montreal. Joining us was Moreira's mother, who had flown in from Brazil for the week. A of couple days later, the three of us went to the trendy Jell-O Bar club on Ontario Street, where it was salsa night. We all danced until three in the morning.

Laliberté was generous to Moreira's family; he paid for her mother to fly in frequently to visit her grandchildren. He also continued to employ one of her brothers in a high-up position at Cirque du Soleil for years after they split. Despite all his arguing, he made it a point to be honourable to the extended family of his children.

Mrs. Moreira was a complete contrast to her wiry, dainty daughter. She was slightly overweight, shorter, and looked like she had lived a tough life. The one thing she had in common with my friend was that she was extremely outgoing. After our excursion, she had even downed a few beers like they were water.

Near the end of her trip to Montreal, Mrs Moreira took her daughter aside and told her she thought I was the right guy for her. "He's the one you should be with," Moreira told me her mother said. She'd also said I was "good with kids and kind," and that Moreira needn't look any further. When she told me this we both had a good laugh. We spoke candidly about how there could never be anything between us.

"I'll never date a woman with fake boobs," I told her. "So that rules you out. And you seem to only like men with eight- or nine-figure bank accounts. Mine is minus seven."

Moreira appreciated my sense of humour. She also liked the inordinate amount of freedom we felt with each other and which let us both feel like we didn't have a care in the world. When I was with her, I felt a sense of entitlement. She enjoyed my company, and it was great for my ego to be walking around Montreal with the hottest woman in the city. But I would try to come back down to earth and not get too consumed by that. The key was to realize we were just human beings caught up in our own tiny worlds.

The next weekend that Moreira was alone, she called and asked me to meet her for dinner. Her kids were with Laliberté; my daughter was with her mother. I spent the next few days with Moreira. It was the most memorable and enlightening time I had with her. We went out to a fancy sushi restaurant in Montreal's Plateau district, and during the dinner she received a call from Laliberté. He was asking her to pick up the kids earlier than planned the next day, because he had to fly in his private jet to Vegas on business. A shouting match ensued. Moreira refused his request, telling him, "Your children should be more important than your business. I just don't understand how you can call me on my night off and ask me this. Sorry, but I'm busy."

By now Moreira was fluent in French, and whenever Laliberté called it was the language they conversed in. Most of the other calls she received on her cell were from people who spoke English. I could not help but eavesdrop, because whenever we went out, her phone would ring at least a dozen times.

I asked her if she ever turned the thing off. "No," she replied, "not even when I'm having sex. You never know who might be trying to call. I wish I could turn it off, but with three kids I need to leave it on at all times."

After sushi we headed over to the new "in" spot, Time Supper Club. There was a long line of people at the front door waiting to get in. When we arrived everyone recognized Moreira, and we were able to jump the queue. After being whisked inside, we laughed, drank, and acted like fools in the club's VIP area. We danced and grinded against each other all night. The place was hopping. That night she introduced me to a mutual friend of hers and Laliberté's, and, while Moreira continued dancing the night away, I took a seat with this woman and got a crash course on what actually happened in Moreira and Laliberté's relationship.

The woman had been good friends with them both until the split. She had decided to sever ties with them, because they were both consuming all of her time with their problems. "They both were acting like spoiled children. They didn't show any class. I don't feel anything for either of them. From now on, I'm staying away from them.

"The fact of the matter is that both of them have severe emotional problems and live life with the intention of making the other miserable," she said. "Both of them act like they're twelve years old. The saddest part of it all is how much the kids suffer. They get shuttled back and forth like no one's business. If it keeps up, they're going to get dizzy. They need a stable environment. Both Rizia and Guy seem more interested in partying than being parents. Not to say they're bad parents, but I'm certain that neither of them really knew what they were getting into when they had three kids."

Then, the woman divulged the sizzler. I had asked her outright why Moreira and Laliberté had had three kids without ever getting married. The woman's explanation was startling. "They were supposed to get married two years ago, but it was called off because they couldn't agree on a place to live," she said. "Rizia wanted to move back to Brazil, and Guy wanted to bring the kids up in Montreal. If Rizia would have agreed to stay in Montreal, I'm certain they would still be together and married."

This was the first I had heard of any wedding plans. I couldn't wait to ask Moreira if this was all true, but it would have to wait till the next day. She was still swivelling her hips on the dance floor and drinking one shot of vodka after another. Her boyfriend Peter, the lawyer, showed up around one o'clock in the morning. He was a fine specimen —polite, but without much of an edge. He had style and was extremely outgoing on the dance floor, where his dance moves and his smile were laid back. He ordered shots for all of us, even though Moreira's entourage had grown to eight people by then.

"I don't think Rizia knows what she's doing," the friend told me while Moreira and her boyfriend were on the dance floor, shaking their bodies. "She's only been separated for a few months, and already she's had numerous boyfriends. I feel bad for Peter. How in the world will he ever keep up with a man like Guy Laliberté? That's going to be an issue for him and anyone else who dates Rizia. She has extremely expensive tastes. One would need a vault of cash to support a girlfriend with her tastes; she doesn't buy anything that's not top of the line."

A friend of of his who was with us that night at Time didn't hesitate to give me his opinion. "I don't think Peter's serious about Rizia at all," he said. "I think he gets a kick out of the fact that he's dating Guy Laliberté's ex. Peter is good friends with Guy. I wouldn't be surprised if they've already exchanged notes. I give this relationship a couple of months, at most, before Peter bails.

"Peter may not have the cash Guy does, but he's certainly well off. And like Guy, he's a player with the ladies. He gets bored quickly and then moves on to the next woman. I think Rizia knows this but is probably trying to use Peter to make Guy jealous. I don't think it will happen. Guy probably has four women at his house right now, giving him their full attention. I'm sure he's not at home missing Rizia; I'll bet anything I have on that."

By the end of the night I had witnessed enough at Time to make me think twice about coming back. Everyone in the club seemed completely stoned out of their minds. Yet everyone respectfully coexisted—the druggies, the fags, the leather set, and the snobs. Moreira seemed to mix well with each of the groups. Decadent as it seemed, she told me she enjoyed it because there was a certain honesty to it.

"There's no discrimination here," she told me. "There's not one person in the club who doesn't feel good. Everyone is out to have a good time and everyone is treated equally." I was sceptical about her line about equal treatment. It was easy for her to say that, from the club's exclusive roped-off VIP section.

When we got back to her apartment, we had drinks with Peter and a couple of other friends who joined us. After about an hour the party wrapped up and everyone left, including Peter. I felt weird, wondering how he felt that I was staying the night while he went home.

"Maybe he'll get jealous," Moreira said. "It might do him some good. I don't want to throw myself at him; that would ruin it for me. He needs to feel a bit of tension, a bit of insecurity. Peter's a good guy, but he's a bit lost in his life. I'm not sure he's the right one for me, because I like a man with a strong mind. He's a bit too wrapped up in his own life. It's good that he went home, because then he won't be overconfident. When men get too confident, it's bad. They start taking advantage of the situation."

It was at that moment that I realized how masterful a manipulator Moreira could be. That she bragged about it made me a bit wary. I wondered how she talked about me behind my back. From then on, I was more on guard. This woman was capable of cutting people down with words better than anyone I had seen. It began to make sense to me why Laliberté wanted to have nothing to do with her. He had probably had enough of her games.

"Rizia acted like a kid around Guy; that's why it didn't last," one of Rizia's close friends told me. "But what can you expect? There's a fifteen-year age difference between them. You get what you pay for in life, and in this case Rizia was still pretty much a kid when Guy chose her. He should have thought it out more carefully. As tough as Guy can be, like all other men he has weaknesses when it comes to women."

To cap off that fun filled weekend, we went out that Monday

night to a popular club on Saint Laurent Street that Guy owned with his brother Jean. Laliberté had invested in several business ventures run by family and close friends. A year later he would finance the refurbishing of the old 1234 Club on rue de la Montagne, or Mountain Street, again with his brother Jean. Mondays were the most popular night at the Upper Club, when it drew Montreal's hipsters, artists, and fashion people.

As soon as we entered, Moreira became the focus of attention. Jean Laliberté greeted her and kissed her on both cheeks. Several other acquaintances of hers came up to her to talk. On this night I saw one more important thing about Moreira that would be crucial later on. Whenever she got the chance that night, she took shots at Laliberté. I thought it was pretty low, considering a lot of the people she talked to in the club were mutual friends of theirs. This night I learned how she was capable of stabbing someone in the back when they weren't looking. I eavesdropped on a conversation she had with someone who worked for Laliberté at Cirque. She gave him a mouthful as she told him how Guy doesn't support her, how he cheated so many times on her, and how much she wanted something bad happen to him for all the terrible things he did to her.

"Rizia comes off as sweet and innocent," a close friend of hers says. "She's the furthest thing from it. She's the type of person who will do anything and use anyone to get what she wants. As nice as she seemed, I know so many people who got tired of her dishonest games and dumped her as a friend. She thinks they all left because of her fallout from Guy. Nothing could be further than the truth."

I heard from Moreira how she valued the importance of dreams for people whose lives were hard. She insisted that if she became rich she would enrich the lives of many others. "I like to share," she said. "I think I deserve to be rich, but I won't be like other people who don't put it to good use. I want to help people."

I was far from convinced. Whenever we went out, she expected other people to pick up her tab. I found it to be a bit selfish, considering how much money she was getting a month from Laliberté.

"I guarantee you, a lot of the money she was getting each month from Guy was not going to the kids," a close friend of Moreira says. "Whenever it was Guy's turn to take the kids, Rizia was on the next plane to some exotic place like Ibiza or Brazil. She wasn't working; I don't think she has ever worked. That money had to be coming from somewhere."

But the more I watched Moreira, the stronger was my impression that the jet-set life was not just about glamour for her. More than anything else, she seemed to want friends she could trust. Although she liked to travel more than anyone I had ever met, she blamed that on her emotional problems.

"I can't still she admitted. "Guy's the same way. We like movement; being in the same place all the time gets boring. I feel fortunate that I'm able to travel a lot."

Despite her frequent long periods away from the kids, Moreira was a caring mother. Whenever I saw her with the children, she showed them nothing but affection, focus, and love. And they reciprocated; they stuck to their mother like glue. The thing that impressed me most about the children was the normal life they were leading despite their father's vast wealth. Aside from the fact that Laliberté wanted to have his children implanted with microchips in case they got kidnapped, everything else around them seemed normal. They played extremely well with other kids and respected that they could not get whatever they wanted. Their bedrooms had toys but not an excessive amount of them. Considering they had a father who was a billionaire, they were far from spoiled.

Another character trait I appreciated in Moreira was her humour. On the retreat I had organized that summer, she had driven her silver Mercedes by accident into a muddy swamp. I was with her, and she had ignored my advice to not drive into a particular wooded area in the dark, during a heavy rain. The car got stuck and was covered in mud. Many other people would have gotten angry or frustrated, but not her. She laughed uncontrollably. She thought it was hilarious. We ended up sleeping in the car, and the next morning we got a few strong men to push it out.

Despite her faults and deceptions, no one I have ever met liked to joke around and have a good laugh as much as Moreira. This is something I'll always remember her for. The times we had together were some of the most fun I've ever had in my life. There were happy moments and happy pictures, especially during our excursions to the countryside.

But back in Montreal, our friendship started to deteriorate. Once Moreira realized I would not call my uncle, the Supreme Court justice, and ask him for the favour she wanted, she became distant.

Shortly after her lawyer took her on as a client, he told me "She exaggerates everything to her benefit, she's always late, and all she's after is to get as much money from Guy as possible," he told me. "Whatever I suggest, it's not good enough. Whatever Guy offers is not good enough. We have a major problem here. I think she's more interested in making Guy's life miserable than she is in settling the case."

Needless to say, her client relationship with her lawyer would soon end up in shambles like it had with her previous lawyer. He was furious about Moreira's deceits. He said she was uncooperative and changed her story almost every day. She also owed him a lot of money, which he claims he has not received to this day. Things got really ugly, he adds, when she reported him to the Quebec Bar Association, accusing him of undermining her case and sexually harassing her.

"She's nuts, completely nuts," her lawyer said. "After all I did for her, she made up stories to try to ruin my career. She's been the biggest nightmare client of my life. I never want to talk to her again. I feel bad for Guy. I met him several times during court procedures, and he really seemed like a sincere person. She must have done things to him to piss him off similar to what she did to me. In the end, I believe in karma, and I believe everyone gets what they deserve."

Moreira frequently barged in on Laliberté, despite warnings from him and his lawyers to stay away. She'd often show up unannounced and confront him on issues regarding their children and their acrimonious separation. One night, when the three children were with Laliberté, Moreira and I were having dinner at the new, luxurious town house he had just bought her on Olivier Avenue in Westmount. During dessert, she got up, picked up her Sony video camera, and said she was heading over to Laliberté's house. I talked her out of going to spy on Laliberté, who she was convinced was having a party while his kids were sleeping in the house.

"I'm sure there are lots of drugs, alcohol, and women there," she said. After she agreed not to go, we went dancing at her regular hangout, Time Supper Club. We met her old friend David there, a single dad who claims he used to be a member of the Israeli Mossad. David and she talked in a corner for more than an hour. I suspected something was up.

The next afternoon I got a call from Moreira urging me to come over. She told me she had something incredible to show me. When I arrived at her home, she took out her camera and started playing a video she had recorded a few hours earlier. It was quite shocking. The video showed that she had walked into Laliberté's home while filming.

Alcohol bottles were strewn everywhere. The three kids were sleeping in a bedroom, totally oblivious to the party that had obviously been going on while they slept. When Moreira reached the master bedroom, she opened the doors. Inside, the scene was something that might have been conceived by the most creative of Hollywood scriptwriters. Laliberté was lying in bed with whisky and vodka bottles all around the room. Suddenly, two heads popped out from underneath the blankets. Both were women who Moreira had seen before with her ex. One was a stripper whose sister was a well-known Montreal model.

Incredibly, Laliberté kept his cool during the entire episode. "Good morning, Rizia," he said. "How are you, Rizia?" This convinced me that Laliberté was not the violent, shouting monster Moreira had tried to portray to me. He was obviously a party animal, however, and that is what she claims had ruined their relationship. She told Laliberté she was going to use the video to discredit him in court. But the court, after viewing it, refused to let it be admissible because it had been filmed illegally. Laliberté could have charged Moreira for entering his home unlawfully, but he didn't.

I remained a casual friend to Moreira for the next couple of years, and then we lost contact when I moved to New York City in late 2005. Three years later, during a visit to Montreal, our paths crossed once again. I met her in Westmount Square, coming out of a clinic where I was undergoing treatment for a back injury. She noticed me and stopped me.

We talked for almost an hour and caught up on each other's lives. She wouldn't stop talking about her issues with Laliberté: "I spent ten years by his side and ended up with nothing. It's not fair." she told me.

After all these years she was still filled with so much resentment. I wondered to myself why this woman, thirty-four years old in 2008, couldn't just get a life. Her preoccupation was still with Laliberté.

She hadn't worked a day in her life and had maids, cooks, and a beautiful home and was still so unhappy. I told her it might be better if she gave it up and moved on.

* * *

I had already spent hundreds of hours advising and listening to Rizia ramble on about her case. Normally, my consulting fee is a minimum of $75 an hour. In this case Rizia used me as much as she could to further her own cause. She never offered me a dime for my time. She expected everyone around her to do things for her for free while she benefited from Guy's largesse.

She also found out I had accepted $400 from her lawyer for recommanding her, and she hit the ceiling. She accused me of being paid much more and asked me if Guy was financing me to spy on her. When I told her I had only been paid a paltry sum, she refused to believe me and started bad-mouthing me around Montreal. I told her if she continued to yap I would have no choice but to launch a slander suit against her.

Her accusation that Guy was paying me was completely false. I was not the first person she accused Guy of paying off. She once told me she thought he paid off her previous set of lawyers and was worried that he was going to try the same thing with this one. When I told her she's overly paranoid and that paying off lawyers in Québec is highly illegal, she calmed down. She explained to me that in her native Brazil such practices were common and that she supposed the same thing went on in Canada. When I told her definitely not, she refused to believe it. She insisted that Guy had the power and money to influence everyone, from the lawyers to the court stenographer to the judge, in order to get the judgment he wanted. As for my $400 fee, which worked out to less than ten cents an hour by the numbers, I told her it was between me and the lawyer and that I was entitled to receive at least something to cover my expenses for all the time I had invested. It was an insult to the numerous years I had put in as a professional consultant. I explained to her how in the past I had worked as a consultant for the likes of Yale University, American civil-rights lawyer David Boies, and the E Channel for excellent remuneration. She told me she disagreed. She used the excuse that because we were friends she didn't feel it was necessary to pay me. What a load of crap. Try using that line in today's competitive world, I told her, and see how far it takes you.

Because we didn't see eye to eye, we never broached the subject again. We continued to be friends, but our relationship never felt the same to me. It became very clear that she wanted to use me and my connections without having to pay a penny. This was not conducive to my well being considering the fact that I had a baby daughter I had to feed and clothe. No one was paying me thousands of dollars a month in child support. Not that I expected much from Rizia, but the fact it never dawned on her to offer me a penny for my time and effort disgusted me. Any respect I had for her was completely lost.

# 14

During their ten years together, Moreira was many things to Laliberté—his lover, party companion, confidante, and mother to his children.

"There are people starving in these recessionary times and this woman has the nerve to complain about being given half a million bucks to renovate her new house, "a source says." I was not impressed by her at all. It became more and more obvious how greedy she is, and that all she was out to accomplish was to extract as much cash from Guy as she could. It's an insult to people who work hard for what they get."

"She's a master manipulator who is very clever," a close friend of Moreira's says. She was determined to get at him any way she could. It started to drive Laliberté nuts.

Several of their close friends were concerned about how Rizia's and Guy's issues would affect the couple's three children.

"I can't believe how long it has dragged on; it's been years," says

José. I think there's so much bad feeling between the two that no matter what happens in the end, it will never be just water under the bridge. They'll probably keep fighting each other until one of them dies. I've never seen two people fight as much as they do, especially so many years after they separated. It's not normal.

"Most of Rizia's stories about Guy have been discounted because she's proven to be completely obsessed with him. Guy, on the other hand, has proven to be a class act throughout the entire ordeal. I am far from impressed with how she has handled everything."

Since Laliberté, Moreira had dated a string of men before becoming involved in a serious relationship with a wealthy Montreal businessman. Herbert Black was in his early sixties when he met Moreira. He had long been one of Montreal's most eligible and handsome bachelors and had dated a string of beautiful and glamorous women. Before Moreira, his long list of girlfriends had included the stunning socialite, Larissa Abrahamian, then twenty-nine years old, who was at Black's side almost 24/7. Clearly, Black had a penchant for women young enough to be his daughter or even granddaughter.

Black dated Moreira for two years, starting in 2004. Long after they broke up, Black started paying her legal bills. Known as Montreal's scrap-metal king, he had amassed a multi-million-dollar fortune and could afford to be generous.

Black's involvement was somewhat controversial however. He used to be close friends with Laliberté and was often spotted with him at trendy Montreal restaurants. Laliberté was also a regular passenger in Black's state-of-the-art helicopter. Now Black was turning his back on his old friend as he came to share Moreira's point of view.

Known to be an amazing spin doctor, Black told the media how outraged he was by Quebec's marriage laws. When a member of the media asked him his thoughts about Laliberté, he got visibly upset.

Black had already earned a reputation as a crusader and was no stranger to big court cases. Back in 2000, he was the catalyst in one of the most notorious antitrust cases in American history, in which a class-action lawsuit against Sotheby's and Christie's auction houses won US$ 152 million.

"Rizia must be the only woman on the planet who can convince an ex-boyfriend to keep paying her bills," José says. "Her relationship with Black was her most bizarre relationship to date; he was almost twice her age. I guess she became obsessed with any man who was worth at least hundreds of millions. No matter how much money Black had, he was still no match for Guy, who was worth around four times as much.

Moreira tried to throw more egg on Laliberté's face by telling close friends that he was doing the same thing to his current lover and partner that he had done to her. Laliberté had had two other children with Montreal fashion model Claudia Barilla.

Laliberté and Barilla lived together in a mansion in Outremont and had  also found their dream home in Hawaii—a $29-million, ten-bedroom estate at the Big Island's Mauna Kea Resort. When they bought it in 2007, it was the most expensive purchase ever by a home buyer in Hawaii, smashing the previous highest purchase of $24 million back in 2006 by a wealthy family from Europe.

When Laliberté hooked up with the stunning Barilla, he apparently promised her he would cut back on his notorious party lifestyle. It was one of the conditions she imposed if they were going to have children together. He already had the three children with Moreira, but he was intent on having more.

"Guy has always been clear that the wants to have lots of children," says "Alice," a friend who prefers to use a fictitious name. "When he meets women like Claudia and Rizia, he visualizes how the children would look. And like in his business, he's always right on. Guy has amazing foresight. He goes with his gut feeling, and he's usually never wrong."

Close friends of Laliberté and Barilla confirm that the jet-set couple had problems. It appears that like Moreira, Barilla became impatient with his refusal to marry her. According to a close friend, "Claudia told him to marry her for the sake of their two children or she'd leave him. She and Guy have had problems and are trying to work them out." The friend goes on to say that Barilla was no innocent victim. "Like Moreira, she certainly has her own demons to deal with. Guy has given her everything her heart could dream of, but it doesn't appear to be enough. If they split, it will cost Guy millions."

Laliberté didn't deny Moreira's current round of allegations against him. He had no intention of marrying Barilla. Marriage wasn't for him and he didn't believe in it.

As I watched all this, and as the owner of one of the biggest celebrity gossip websites in the world, I began to feel determined to feed to the world the story that I had been close to for so many years. I didn't feel I owed Moreira anything, especially once I realized she'd used me to get closer to my uncle, the Supreme Court justice. I wasn't seeking revenge, but I wouldn't go out of my way to defend her.

In fact, the few times I met Laliberté, he seemed to be one of the most humble, personable, and least assuming persons I'd ever met. One time I bumped into him at Cafeteria, one of his favourite hangouts on trendy Saint-Laurent Boulevard. He was with a group of about ten friends. I was sitting at the next table, and at one point during the night I got into a lengthy conversation with him. I told him I had been a busker years back, and he regaled me with one story after another about how he used to enjoy performing on the streets when he first started out.

"It was so simple, so pure, and so much fun," he told me. "When I busked, they were some of the happiest days of my life. I once worked a regular job and after three days realized that it wasn't for me. Since then I've always worked for myself. I wasn't the type who would be able to adapt to a regular work environment."

The waitress serving me at Cafeteria was the same one who served Laliberté and his entourage. I asked her how she felt serving one of only six billionaires in Quebec. "Guy is one of us," she told me. "No matter how much money he makes, he's one of the nicest people out there. He has a heart of gold. Every time he comes in here, he foots the bill for all his friends, buys the staff here shot after shot, and leaves a tip of almost the same amount as the bill. Lots of rich people come in here who have big egos and attitude. Not Guy; he's never let success go to his head. He's always stayed the same simple Guy, the good friend I met years ago when he barely had two pennies to rub together."

Next, I asked the waitress about Moreira. She said she had met her several times. "Whenever she comes in here, she walks in as if she owns the place," she said. "She wants to have special treatment and wants everyone to cater to her as if she's royalty. She loves money and seems to only have time for people with lots of cash or people she could use for her own purposes. She's the complete opposite of Guy, who, despite all his money, has stayed pretty much the same. Rizia is only out for his cash. She should think twice about what she's doing, because everyone sees through her. I don't know how she can live with herself."

After listening to the waitress ramble on about the ex-couple, the situation became clearer to me than ever and my resolve grew. Moreira was interested solely in her own security, even more than that of her children. It looked as if she used her children as an excuse to stake a claim to Laliberté's wealth.

Laliberté, on the other hand, never lost his emotional connection to ordinary people, such as those on the streets who he had entertained many years ago. He never looked down on anyone, especially if they were poor. He always looked at his good fortune as being a gift.

"Guy never let it get to his head," says José. "He never forgets where he came from and has used his good fortune to make other people's lives better. Just the thousands of people he created jobs for at Cirque du Soleil over the years is incredible. He is directly responsible for helping many people realize their dreams and lead better and richer lives. Rizia, on the other hand, is out for herself.

# 15

In the past I had tangled with much bigger and well I known fish than Moreira and Laliberté, including The Church of Scientology, Michael jackson, Britney Spears, and even the entire fashion industry, when I posed undercover as a male model to expose the industry's injustices. In my posts I made it clear that nothing had stopped me in the past, and nothing was about to stop me now. I was prepare to deal with any consequences that came my way; I would fight them to my last penny.

In my posts I referred to Moreira as Quebec's version of Heather Mills, Paul McCartney's ex-wife. Mills attempted to take McCartney for almost everything he had after they unceremoniously split in May 2006. In fact I found the similarities between Mills and Moreira disturbing. Both were ex-models, both were heavily into natural medicine and alternative remedies, and both had a long history of hobnobbing with some of the world's richest jet-setters. The only major difference between the two fortune hunters was that Mills was able to get McCartney to put a ring around her finger.

"Heather Mills and Rizia Moreira are two peas in a pod," says journalist Esmond Choueke. "They were both interested in one thing: marrying very rich and then cashing out. Both of them tried to get public sympathy after their relationships dissolved, but they were unsuccessful. The public saw through them, and their plans completely backfired. They were seen as being relentless gold-diggers."

Before I posted, I had consulted with one of Laliberté's closest friends, Juliette Powell, a former MusiquePlus VJ with whom I had become good friends in New York. Powell urged me not to write anything about his family life because there were children involved. I promised her I would not mention any of the kids' names in anything I wrote. At the time, I had no idea I would turn around and pen a book about Laliberté. To keep true to my promise to Powell, I have refrained from mentioning the children by name in this book. Although even without Powell's advice, I wouldn't have mentioned their names. I'm a father myself, and I would never want my daughter's name mentioned publicly until she was of legal age.

Perhaps the most controversial post of my series was when I described how Moreira thought about knocking off Laliberté after she found out he was seeing supermodel Naomi Campbell. An old friend of ours had warned me that Moreira was losing her mind after hearing that Laliberté intended to propose to Campbell. Apparently he had told this to a friend. My friend told me Moreira wanted to kill him. No matter how hard Moreira was willing to fight against Laliberté, I couldn't see her actually going through with an attempt to murder him. I refused to believe it was in her character to pull off such a gruesome act, and obviously she had said it during the heat of the moment. If I thought she was serious about carrying through an attempt on Laliberté's life, I would have gone straight to the police.

The response to my posting was once again in Laliberté's favour. No one seemed to be shedding tears for a woman who seemed intent on becoming extremely wealthy without ever having worked a day in her life. Most felt that Moreira knew what she was getting into when she met Laliberté and that he certainly didn't put a gun to her head to have his children.

"Sounds like she tried to do everything to run Guy into the ground," Angela commented on my site. "Go, Guy, Go! Don't let this bitch ruin you!"

During the time I was posting about Moreira and Laliberté, several of their friends contacted me. "Rizia is freaking out over what you're writing," one friend called "Tony" said. "She feels betrayed." I told Tony to tell Moreira that I was just telling it like it is and really had no hard feelings toward her. In fact, I went out of my way to describe how she was an excellent mother, even if she was away from the kids travelling a good portion of the time. I alluded to the fact that many other mothers in the world, like Madonna and Angelina Jolie, were often away from their kids, but it by no means meant they were bad parents. I also mentioned how I found Laliberté to be a stand-up guy and that he always made sure his children were well taken care of.

A close friend of Laliberté contacted me to say how much Laliberté appreciated my balanced views. Alice told me, "He's been following your site every day and is happy that someone finally had the balls to stand up to Rizia and expose her for what she really is. Guy just wants the truth to get out."

Instantly, my site became one of the most talked about in the entire country. My business partner in New York had to increase the site's bandwith to handle the overflow of people logging onto my website.

Afterwards, I gave a forty-five-minute-long interview in French on

CHEQ FM radio in Quebec. It was one of the biggest challenges of my professional career; in the past I had given many interviews to the French media, but never at such great length. The interview turned out to be a great success. Two minutes after it was over, I received an email from the producer of the show asking me to be a regular contributor. It was one of the most flattering and gracious offers I have ever received. I accepted without hesitating.

I knew this would be a first in Quebec City. I don't think there had ever been an Anglophone with his own spot on one of the most notorious French stations in the province. It made me think of Laliberté, how he always seemed to defy the impossible. Perhaps spending so much time covering him was affecting me in a good way.

"Everyone Guy touches, something good usually happens to them," Denis wrote on my website. "He's one of a kind. He doesn't try to keep all the success and glory his way. He likes to spread it better than anyone. Selfish is the last word anyone who knows Guy will use to describe him."

# Part III

# 16

A momentous date on the jet-set social calendar was in the month of June, when Laliberté threw his annual Grand Prix party. It attracted A-listers from all over the world. The Sunday night after the big Formula One race, Laliberté would host a bash at his sprawling mansion in Saint-Bruno that would usually end up lasting a few days. It became the highlight of the year for the world's jet-set crowd. Years later, Laliberté had to move the party to an airport base because of recurring complaints by neighbours about the incredible noise level and wild partying. Everyone who attended was awed.

"I have attended the finest parties all over the world, but nothing that compares to this," says Myra Jones, a Milan-based fashion model who attended several of Laliberté's parties. "Everything you wanted was available at Guy's parties—drugs, the best music spun by famous DJs flown in from Europe and the U.S., and the wildest sex you could ever imagine."

Many people in Laliberté's inner circle worked for months in advance to plan his big bash. One of his close friends "Jake"recalls when Robert De Niro attended in 2001, while in town shooting the film *The Score*, which turned out to be legendary screen star Marlon Brando's last flick before he died. De Niro, who was known for dating beautiful black women, had the time of his life at Laliberté's party.

"I rounded up the hottest black strippers, prostitutes, and models in Montreal and invited them to Guy's party," Jake reveals. "Guy likes to do anything and everything to please his guests. He wants them to have the time of their lives at his parties. If he knows a special guest likes Italian wine, he'll have the most expensive bottles flown in. These are bottles you'd never be able to get at a liquor store in Montreal. Guy pays attention to detail in everything he does, whether it's in his circus or at his amazing parties. And he spares no expense."

Laliberté's mountainside home in Saint-Bruno was an architectural gem. Its security system was one of the most sophisticated in the world, complete with sensors, video cameras, and an alarm system that would go off in a flash if any suspicious activity was occurring inside or outside. Laliberté had his own private lake and immense gardens, filled with rows of tall, centuries-old trees.

Gorgeous women from all over the world were often present, in addition to many of the world's leading entertainment, arts, and business moguls. B-list guests at his parties would be asked to sign confidentiality agreements before being allowed entrance. The fun would usually last several days before Laliberté would instruct his staff to turn on the grounds' sprinkler system, which was the signal that the party was officially over.

"The first time I went to Guy's home I thought I had just entered paradise," says "Abby" a stripper from Las Vegas who was a regular at his parties. "Everything was so classy and so detailed. I have been to mansions in the Hamptons, Greece, and Saint-Tropez; nothing I have seen comes remotely close to Guy's incredible home. It's like being at one the world's greatest wonders.

"Everything was permitted. I tripped out for four days. There were tents, campers, and rooms set up for everyone to sleep in. During the party there were rooms available for people to have sex in. A lot of orgies took place. I should know, because I ended up spending a few days in a camper with a wealthy couple from Georgia who were good friends. They were both into experimenting and used me as their guinea pig. I had sex with both of them during my stay. We also did lots of drugs. It was quite the experience."

Despite Laliberté's worries about police interference at his parties, he refused to lock out his close cop friends. But he made them promise to turn a blind eye to what was happening.

"Essentially it was give-and-take with the police," journalist Esmond Choueke says. "Guy would let them in if they promised to behave and have a good time. Lots of cops party hard when they're off duty. It was a brilliant strategy on Guy's part to make sure the place didn't get busted, since there was so much sex and drugs. He needed to do something to ensure a SWAT team didn't descend on his home in middle of the party. It would have created headlines all over the world. He managed to avoid that."

Nevertheless, there was the threat of Moreira. "Moreira was concerned that a lot of the parties were happening when the kids were in the house, like the time she walked in and filmed him with two women in his bed and the kids in the next room," a close friend of Laliberté's says. "By 2003, there was a lot of heat on Guy to tone it down. He moved the party to the Saint-Hubert airport and in recent years has just had close friends over for the Grand Prix weekend. He got tired of dealing with all the crap involved. Because of previous complaints, he made sure no drugs were in the open, and he put a tight rein on how things were organized. It was a far cry from his parties of a few years back, when everything you can think of was totally out in the open."

One group Laliberté did keep away was Quebec's notorious chapter of the Hell's Angels. Although he casually knew several leading members of the biker gang, he didn't go out of his way to invite them to his parties.

"Guy wanted to make sure that his parties exuded class and went off without any trouble," one of Laliberté's close friends says. "He was never one to try to mix with bikers or undesirables. He knew a lot of them, but in Montreal it's rare to find someone on the party scene who doesn't have some connection to them. I never noticed bikers at his parties; if they were there, they certainly were not wearing leather jackets and leather pants. They would have got in by dressing in more formal attire."

The friend adds that around a thousand of the guests at the main party would leave the grounds of the mansion the following morning, while several dozen would be invited to stay on and enjoy the next couple of days.

"The guests who stayed on were treated like kings," the friend says. "They were treated to luxury: the best food, the best drink, and a relaxing time in the sun. The weather in Montreal that time of year is usually amazing. Everyone's in a great mood because the sun is out and summer is in the air. With the Grand Prix race and the beautiful weather combined, Guy could not choose a better time of year. But then again, Guy's timing is usually impeccable."

Laliberté's trademark grand entrance to his party would be in the early hours of the next morning, when he'd appear high atop a platform that was visible to the huge crowd. He'd be shirtless, with the huge tattoo on his back visible to everyone. Within a few seconds he'd start breathing fire out of his mouth, the way he used to when he was a busker in the early 1980s. It was the rallying cry of his old artist self. The crowd would go wild, and a huge cheer would engulf the mansion's compound.

Before Laliberté performed there would be an array of Cirque du Soleil-type performers strutting their stuff, including acrobats, jugglers, clowns, masseuses, and fortune tellers. But none could spark the pulse of the crowd with the same intensity as Laliberté. He was a more vivid and charismatic performer than any other.

"When Guy would come out and do his incredible fire-breathing, we'd all go crazy," says "Ginette" a regular at his parties. "The entire place would erupt. It showed us how truly artistically talented our host was. Even with all the sex, drugs, and everything else going on, the thing I remember most was Guy's fire-breathing. It was a beautiful and spectacular site."

Eden Rothman was invited to the party as the guest of her then-boyfriend, who owned a post-production film studio in New York. It was her first trip to Montreal. She refers to it as her best trip ever. Rothman says her only regret was that she didn't bring a video camera because everything was so spectacular, and her recollections probably don't do the party justice.

"After we checked in, we saw there were naked women at the entrance holding parrots," she says. "It was incredible. There were different rooms all over the property with different music playing. The main DJ on the floor was incredible, and people were dancing as if they were having the time of their lives. Everyone was friendly and acted as if we were all on the same level. No one was really paying attention to any stars who were there. It was all one big happy family.

"The best part was when one of the DJs asked me if I wanted to go with him to a special tent set up for couples wanting to have sex. My boyfriend overheard his proposition and said, 'Only if I'm allowed to join in.' The three of us ended up having sex for more than two hours. It was very special, very spiritual, and very enlightening. It was the first time I saw my boyfriend make out with a guy. Afterwards he told me how good he felt and said that every man should have sex with another man at least once in his life. I'll never forget how he said it; he really meant it. It brought us closer together than ever before. And he said he had enjoyed watching me have sex with another man just as I enjoyed watching him. We're not together anymore, but we'll keep this special memory until the day we die. I'm sure many people who attended Guy's parties will keep the memories ingrained in their minds forever."

A well-known business executive in Montreal says attending Guy's party was one of the highlights of his life. It had taken him three years to finally get an invitation, when finally a friend he had in common with Laliberté arranged it. He said people kept coming over to introduce themselves all night. From the moment he arrived, he was impressed with every detail.

"I've travelled all over the world but have never experienced anything like Guy's party," he says. "In fact, if it had not ended in the wee hours of the next morning, I could have easily stayed another month. The people and the atmosphere was just amazing. Everyone was in a great mood, and each direction you turned, there was something incredible going on. I occasionally smoke pot, but that night I must have had twelve joints, which were being passed around like candy. I also did several lines of coke. It felt great to be so fucked up in such an amazing atmosphere. It took me several weeks to recuperate, but I didn't have a single regret. It was the greatest night of my life."

A recognizable supermodel I had met while writing my book about the fashion industry says the Grand Prix party at Laliberté's home in 2002 was one of the greatest to-dos she's ever attended. She remembers the evening careening between extremes of glamour and absurdity.

"There was not one person in there who didn't believe they were one of life's privileged ones," she says. "It rocked from the moment you arrived until the moment you left. If it had gone on another few hours, I don't think I would have made it out alive. I did more coke and ecstasy that night than probably in my entire life. I didn't want it to end. And neither did the other thousand people who attended. I've been to so many events and functions—it's part of the business—but I was never at anything like this. Guy knows how to bring you in to his place and take you on a wild, unimaginable journey, just like he does with his circus."

Former swimsuit model and *Playboy* covergirl Angie Everhart attended Laliberté's party the same summer she was shooting the film *Wicked Minds* in Montreal. Everhart, who is a notorious jet-setter and former addict who has dated the likes of Prince Albert II of Monaco and Sylvester Stallone, says the moment you walked through the front doors at Laliberté's mansion, you immediately felt you belonged and were completely transformed. She says there are other parties around the world that jet-setters rave about, but nothing compares to the bash Laliberté threw.

"I loved it," Everhart says. "It was beyond crazy; it was complete insanity for hours. Everyone was so beautiful and so free. It was as if they all dumped their personal baggage at the door and let themselves go. And when Guy made his grand entrance spitting fire out of his mouth, it went from being electric to pandemonium. The music was deafening, which is the way I like it, and the energy was high, really high. If there was a straight person in the house, they must have freaked out watching everyone else trip. They would have thought they were the one on drugs."

Many of the guests brought Laliberté gifts, although he didn't like receiving them and often gave the items away. He got more pleasure out of giving and watching people enjoy his big gift to them—the party.

"The most incredible thing about Guy was that he always had a huge smile on his face when he saw his guests having a great time," a friend of Laliberté says. "He never likes to receive; he just likes to give, both materially and emotionally. I remember the time when one of his close friends in New York said she couldn't come because finances were tight. He told her he understood, and then the day of the party he surprised her with a limo, a first class plane ticket, and money for an outfit to attend the party. Anyone who knows Guy will agree that he never got more excited than he did when seeing the people he cared about being happy. When you step into his home, no matter what background you're from, you get treated like royalty."

When the sky would start lighting up with streaks of pink, that would usually mean the party was ending for those who were not in Laliberté's inner circle. Those who were would be invited to keep the action going for several more days. On the menu for the rest of the party were music, laughter, food, drink, and partying in a far more intimate setting. By the time everyone left they had gotten to know each other well.

"Guy's private parties were even better than his big bashes," says "Rachelle," a stripper friend of Laliberté's who says she was flown in from Montreal to several of his bashes throughout the years. "They were more intimate and more exciting. The DJs were always the best. A lot of times Alain Vinet from Montreal was spinning the records; he's my favorite DJ in the world. And often you'd see the most outrageous acts perform; some were in Cirque, and some weren't. But they would all be very avant-garde and exciting to watch."

"I made contacts that I'll keep for life," Denis says. "I could never figure out how Guy managed to get so many people from different parts of the world to attend. It completely blew my mind. One afternoon when we were all sitting around drinking and relaxing in the sun, I met a woman who had travelled all the way from Ecuador. She said she met Guy in Las Vegas at a breakfast diner, and they became good friends. Guy is probably the only person in the world who could be in a room for less than five minutes and get to know everyone present and remember all their names. He loves people more than anything. It's one of his greatest qualities."

Laliberté told friends that his lavish parties were a tribute to them. He wanted people to have a 1960s feeling of freedom but with a modern twist. He had a calm assurance that whatever happened at his parties was right.

"He took a giant risk with all the sex, booze, and drugs," says "Ted" a friend of Laliberté's. "It could have all collapsed in his face so easily. It would have taken just one incident like a drug overdose or a woman saying she was raped, and he would have been vilified. Yet the measures he took to avoid anything like this were far from great. Sure, he had lots of security and staff on site, but they couldn't monitor everything that was going on; it would have been impossible. He put his faith in his friends, and they never disappointed him. I never even saw a fight break out, although there were lots of guys who were there with their wives doing wife swapping or having fun with other women. It was a real anything-goes atmosphere. No one seemed to object."

A close female friend of his remembers the time she asked Laliberté how many years he intended to keep his parties going. Laliberté, who was stretched out with his arms behind his head watching the sky, responded, "Until I don't have a pulse." The woman, part of Laliberté's party planning team, lay beside him topless. She says that unlike with almost every other man present, she wasn't at all on Laliberté's sexual radar.

"Everyone thinks Guy sleeps with every woman he looks at," she says. "Maybe he does. I can only talk about my own experience; I've been friends with him for almost nine years and not once has he stepped out of bounds. He treats me like a queen. So many of us are just his close friends. We're the people he calls on each year to help him organize the party and to help him plan all the details. One thing about Guy is he knows how to make a woman feel special. He would never try anything on a woman unless she consented. He shows class all the way. I'm extremely grateful to him for that."

One of the most bizarre stories I came across while researching this book came from an L.A. model who spent every cent she had to attend Guy's Grand Prix party. It took her years to make it to his guest list; she got in after befriending a Hollywood producer who she knew had been friends with Laliberté. She said she bought four designer outfits, got her hair straightened at the same Beverly Hills salon where Paris Hilton gets her hair done, and bought herself a $6,000 boob job. All that before airfare, hotel, and travel money. She says she spent over $20,000 in all. She remembers showing up to Laliberté's party with scars and red marks on her remodeled chest. When she returned to L.A. a week later, she considered filing for personal bankruptcy. But her misfortune would be turned around through a person she had befriended at the party.

"Through friends, I had heard so much about Guy's incredible parties," she says. "I had to get on the guest list for at least one of them. After my producer friend who knew him called me, I spent weeks preparing. I wanted to stand out. I looked at it as an opportunity of a lifetime; I didn't want to go and not turn heads. I invested all the money I had and maxed out all my credit cards. When I arrived at the party it was everything and more than I expected. I met Guy, and he was so incredibly down to earth. When it was over, reality sank in. I had just gone broke over this one crazy night. When I returned to L.A., I couldn't pay off my debts and was just about to declare personal bankruptcy.

"A couple of weeks later a man I had exchanged business cards with at the party called me. He had told me that he produced commercials for a major network, and I had talked to him for around an hour about how I wanted to break into the acting business. When he called me in L.A., he asked me to audition for a national TV ad for a new hair product company. I ended up getting the gig and getting paid very well, enough to clear my debts and then some. A couple of months later I landed a network TV pilot. My career started taking off because I took the risk of flying to Montreal to attend the party. What looked like a potentially disastrous decision turned into the greatest career move I ever made."

While thousands of people have enjoyed the extravagance of Laliberté's renowned parties, many others have wondered how much Laliberté doled out for them. Rumours on the Internet suggest he spends from hundreds of thousands all the way to $10 million. A former Cirque executive claims Laliberté's parties were budgeted into Cirque's marketing plans. He claims the parties usually cost $3 million but were a wise investment on Laliberté's part.

"No matter how amazing the parties were, I know for a fact they would never have taken place if Guy did not see a big return on the investment," the former executive says. "Not to say I want to take any credit away from him. He's a master party thrower—better than Hugh Hefner, better than any Oscar party. Nothing has ever compared to the type of party Guy throws.

"How does he make money off it? It's simple: he invites some of the most influential and richest people in the world and treats them like kings. They go back to their countries and spread the word how nice and incredible Guy is. When Cirque tours their respective countries they open every door for Guy, which in turn guarantees Cirque's success there. It's a brilliant marketing and networking plan, maybe the most elaborate ever in the entertainment business.

"There's no way I can sit here, look you in the eye, and tell you he does it strictly out of the goodness of his heart. Sure, he loves to see his friends have a great time. But there have to be ulterior motives involved; no one, not even Guy, does something like this without expecting something back in return. And why shouldn't he receive something back? He deserves it, especially for being able to make so many people happy. Just the smiles on people's faces are what make the whole extravaganza worth it, whether it costs three or one hundred million."

Laliberté's expensive taste in parties extends to the glitzy premieres he throws for new Cirque du Soleil productions. In November 2008, when the U.S. was already deep into an economic downturn, Laliberté spared no expense for the opening night party for the premiere of magician Criss Angel's Cirque show called *Believe*. After investing a reported $100 million in Angel's spectacular magician-meets-Cirque production, Laliberté dished out another half million for the opening night bash.

The extravaganza was for Angel, the show's cast and crew, and the more than three thousand ticket holders who attended the opening night's 7 PM and 10 PM performances. Everyone got in for free and walked out with a commemorative *Believe* dog tag necklace. Numerous stars attended, including Angel's girlfriend, *Playboy* playmate Holly Madison, and former heavyweight champion Mike Tyson.

The details of the party were breathtaking. Guests were given complementary chair massages, flavoured tobacco at a hookah lounge, like MAC makeup kits, and imported cigars. Crimson-coloured boxes of chocolates were handed out, each filled with gold and silver foil wrapped imported chocolates with "Criss Angel: *Believe*" written across them. Food stations across the pool deck served up mouthwatering dishes like miso-marinated sea bass, seafood paella, and full-size T-bone steaks. There was also *foie gras* and *saumon fumé*, to keep Cirque true to its French Canadian roots.

Other opening-night Cirque bashes in previous years had also left their mark in the showbiz world. In New York a few years earlier, Laliberté had wowed more than three thousand party revellers following the premiere of Cirque du Soleil's 2003 production, *Varekai*. Guests left their outerwear at a coat check staffed by fairies, while drinks were served by Greek gods, and a pink and orange sea urchin in flippers mingled with guests. A team of forty creative designers and stylists had transformed a parade of actors, dancers, and servers into characters from Greek myths. "It's sort of an underworld garden look," event planner Gustavo Marcus said of it.

"Every time Guy has a premiere, he invests a lot in the opening night party," the former Cirque executive says. "It's a brilliant marketing strategy. There's no media person who attends one of these events that will ever dare to write a bad word about Cirque du Soleil. They'd never get invited back. Guy makes it a privilege to get into his private openings, and the people invited must show respect if they hope to attend the next one. Amazingly, when Guy dies, I don't know if he'll be remembered more for creating Cirque du Soleil or for his incredible parties. Either way, I don't think anyone will ever match him on either level."

One time Laliberté threw a bash for one of his new productions a bit prematurely. In August 2003, Laliberté launched his most anticipated show ever, *Zumanity*, with a massive blowout party. The next day he announced that the show would be delayed because it wasn't completely polished. He launched it again a month later with an even bigger *soirée.* Yet again, he delayed the show, this time until Christmas.

Laliberté never hesitated to delay a show if he wasn't one hundred percent satisfied with it, no matter how costly it would turn out to be.

Never before had a Cirque show received so much advance publicity. *Zumanity* is the highly controversial Cirque du Soleil production in which two stunning men proclaim their real-life love for each other. Many said it was the most anticipated production of 2003, even more than any Broadway show or Hollywood film. The provocative $50-million production cast real-life lovers Johan Silverhult King and Patrick King as the leads. Laliberté had invited the Kings to perform a twelve-minute audition on his yacht off Saint-Tropez in August 2002, at one of his private parties.

"They asked for something sensual, provocative, and athletic," Patrick King told journalist Steve Friess of the gay newspaper *The Advocate.* "So by the end, we were naked. We had Ivana Trump with her jaw hanging to the floor."

Laliberté's extravagant and exotic parties were reminiscent of the lavish parties thrown by aristocrats during the Roman Empire, where often thousands of guests gorged on exotic specialties on the huge estates they owned. The circus and gladiator contests, in which trained slaves would fight each other until death, were the biggest spectacles of entertainment. Just as the people of the Roman Empire would do anything to attend these lavish affairs as an escape from the hardships and drudgery of their everyday lives, masses of people today are drawn to Laliberté's parties. As Juvenal, the great Roman satirist wrote, "The public . . . longs eagerly for just two things—bread and circuses."

# 17

The day before Laliberté's Grand Prix party in 2000, an incident occurred that I'll never forget. I had been hired to play saxophone with my trio at the Air Canada booth at the Grand Prix event. By then I was a well-established journalist, but I had never stopped pursuing my first passion—playing music. While I was belting out standard jazz tunes like "Summertime" and "Girl From Ipanema," a man wearing dark sunglasses and a beige sunhat and who I thought looked familiar stood to my left, seeming to dig the music.

When we took a break he started talking to me. He spoke in a soft British accent and was extremely pleasant and had a huge smile. He told me how much he loved the saxophone and the great players like Charlie Parker, Art Pepper, and John Coltrane. At one point he dug his fingers deep into my shoulders and told me how much he appreciated my playing.

When I asked him what he did for a living, he replied that he was a musician—a guitarist. I asked him if he was in a group, and he replied that he was. When asked if it was a group I may have heard of, he said, "Even though you're into jazz, you probably would know it. We were a rock-and-roll group, but a lot of our songs have been covered by jazz musicians." This last part of his clue all but gave it away. I thought I might pass out. The man nicknamed the "quiet Beatle," the one who was deep into Indian mysticism, was standing right next to me. I had met numerous celebs over the years, including Princess Diana, Oprah, and Brad Pitt, but never had I been more excited to meet anyone than on that hot summer day, when I talked to George Harrison.

Harrison and I talked for over half an hour, mainly about music and art. He told me how big a race car fan he was and that he was looking forward to the next day's Montreal race with enthusiasm. He had followed the Grand Prix circuit for years, flying to cities around the world in his private Global Express executive jet to take in the action. He would also be attending Laliberté's Grand Prix party this year.

Harrison was the only Beatle who had written an autobiography, *I Me Mine*, published in 1980, and somehow I ended up trying to persuade him to let me update it. I told him about the controversial book I had written a couple of years back about how Kurt Cobain might have been murdered. He said he had heard about it.

"Maybe an added chapter with some controversy in it would be good for my autobiography," he said. "Boy, I could probably sit here and tell you controversial stories for the next decade. There was no shortage of them during my career, especially during my time with the Beatles."

He asked for my phone number and said he'd contact me if he was going to update it or even do another book. "You never know," he said. "Maybe I met you here today for a reason."

I shook hands with Harrison, who then went on his way. My mind was muddled by the end of the conversation, and I had to force myself to keep calm and start my next set. I had just had a one-on-one conversation with one of the greatest musicians ever—the man who had always been my favourite Beatle, my favourite Traveling Wilbury, and my favourite guitarist.

The next day Harrison got drenched in the rain with a hundred thousand other fans who watched German driver Michael Schumacher win the Grand Prix. Harrison probably didn't mind; having grown up in England, he was certainly used to wet weather.

That night Harrison made his way over to Laliberté's party in Saint-Bruno. He was a fan of Cirque du Soleil and was anxious to see its owner, whom he had often bumped into at race tracks all over the world. The two had long shared a mutual admiration. Harrison loved Laliberté's friendly, casual demeanour, and Cirque du Soleil was one of his all-time favourite performing arts groups.

Harrison was one of the two most famous musicians to visit Laliberté's home; the other was Bono, who would serenade Laliberté and a few of his friends with a special private performance several years later.

"Guy always liked hanging out with musicians because music is such a big part of his life," says Denis. "Meeting George Harrison had to be the highlight for him. He talks about it to this day. He'll never forget how humble and gracious a person Harrison was. I've seen him choked up talking about it, and Guy's not one to get choked up too easily."

A couple of years later, Moreira, still with Guy in 2000, recounted to me her reaction when she met Harrison.

"I remember standing next to him and talking to him," she said. "He was a very nice man, and I remember he had a British accent. I would never have recognized him. Even when he told me he used to play in a rock band, I had a tough time figuring out who he was. I felt a bit embarrassed about that. But at Guy's house, there were always famous people over; I had no clue who many of them they were. I was never too up on things like that; people to me are just people."

Later that night, around a campfire at Laliberté's, he and Harrison developed a friendship bond that would last forever. Laliberté, like most young Quebecers who grew up in the 1960s hippie culture, was awestruck. Here was one of his all-time heroes as a guest at his party. He had never appeared more filled with delight.

"I never saw Guy look so happy as that night," Denis says. "He grew up listening to the Beatles. They were his idols. Having George Harrison there was something he could never have imagined in his wildest dreams."

Laliberté and Harrison talked about music, life, and sports cars. Both men were obsessed with race cars, and each was one of only a hundred people who purchased the McLaren F1 road car. They also chatted about a unique idea Harrison proposed to Laliberté on a whim —the Cirque du Soleil doing a Beatles show. Not sure if he was serious or joking, Laliberté instantly replied that it could be a brilliant idea. He joked to Harrison about how cool it would be to see Cirque's clowns and stilt-walkers interpret songs like "Get Back" and "Penny Lane."

By the end of the night, Harrison had made Laliberté promise to visit him at his mansion in England. It was during Laliberté's visit there later on that the pair started to visualize the show and add colourful details. By the end of Laliberté's visit, the two wealthy artists had just about mapped out a show. If nothing ever came of it, at least they would have had a lot of fun talking about it.

Harrison died before his plans with Laliberté could be realized. A year and a half after the England planning session, Harrison became gravely ill. In 1997 he had found a lump on his neck and was diagnosed with throat cancer. He blamed it on his chain-smoking back in the 1960s. The cancer spread, and in May 2001, he underwent an operation at the world-famous Mayo Clinic to remove a growth from one of his lungs. By July 2001, the cancer had spread to his brain. Harrison flew to one of the best clinics in the world, in Switzerland, to receive more radiotherapy. On November 29, 2001, Harrison succumbed to cancer at his L.A. mansion, once owned by the woman I had told him might have been behind Kurt Cobain's death—Courtney Love. Harrison was fifty-eight.

"When Guy found out, he was a complete mess," Denis says. "For the first time in his life, Guy realized that everyone dies. Like Jim Morrison once said, no one gets out of here alive. It had a lasting effect on Guy. He was determined to fulfill the promise he made to his close friend."

Laliberté was going to follow through. He would expand the Beatles legacy with a Cirque show. The tough part was to convince the other surviving Beatles—and the widows of John Lennon and George Harrison—to sign on. The task would be monumental; after the group split, no one had ever managed to get them together in the same room, let alone sign off on a new production. The Beatles' feuds had made world headlines over the years. Laliberté had his work cut out for him, and it would take him more than three years of hard negotiations with the Beatles, their holding company Apple Corps Ltd, and MGM Mirage before contracts were signed.

"Guy had his hands full negotiating with the Beatles," a former Cirque du Soleil executive says. "I think it was the toughest thing he ever did, and it was his biggest achievement. Many before him failed miserably trying to get them together for a project. There were many times during the negotiations when Guy seemed to have had enough. At times the Beatles and their management could be the toughest people in the world to deal with. But I must commend him; he was determined to carry out the dream he shared with George Harrison.

"He was so fond of George and wanted to make him proud. He wanted to share the amazing music of the Beatles with the world through a different artistic form. Not only do I think the final product turned out to be incredible, but I think Guy deserves a medal for making it happen. Can you imagine? The only person in the world who succeeded in getting the Fab Four back together in some shape or form was a man from Quebec, who not too long ago was playing on the streets for a living. That in itself is mind blowing."

Laliberté is the first to admit there were times when it appeared he would lose the biggest battle of his career. The Beatles' mother company had a reputation for being overly litigious in protecting the Beatles legacy. Apple Corps, which had in past years sued EMI Records for skimping on royalties and the Apple Inc computer company for trademark infringement, exercised thorough due diligence on Laliberté and his circus.

In the end, however, Laliberté's tenacity paid off. He showed more integrity and vision than any of the other companies seeking Beatles endorsements. Apple Corps manager Neil Aspinall gave Laliberté a green light. Aspinall became the show's first executive producer, while Dominic Champagne and Cirque founding member Gilles Ste-Croix were brought on as the show's concept creators. Ste-Croix was also the show's director of creation.

"This is a monster show for Vegas," Laliberté said. "The Beatles have been separated for more than thirty years, and this is the first time they are officially endorsing a project about themselves. And they worked with us. This is probably one of the biggest entertainment events of the year. [Both surviving] Beatles [as well as] Yoko Ono,

[and] Olivia Harrison were part of every process for the music and the concept of the show. This show's about love, and through all the process it has been nurtured with love." And so the show would be called *Love*.

Not even Yoko Ono, deemed responsible by many for breaking up the Beatles, stood in Laliberté's way. Most Beatle followers were amazed that Laliberté was able to get Ono's cooperation, because of her long-standing reputation as a control freak and manipulator.

"That Laliberté got all of them in the same room is probably one of the biggest achievements ever in the group's history," Beatles memorabilia collector Dan Newman says. "The Fab Four were at war for decades. I remember when I first heard about the Cirque show on the radio; I thought they were playing some sort of practical joke. When I found out it was true, I still refused to believe it. There was no way in a million years that Yoko Ono and Paul McCartney would agree to work on the same project. They hated each other. Laliberté should become a politician. If he could solve that war, he could probably bring peace to the Middle East and other war-torn parts of the world."

In 2006 *Love* quickly became the most talked about show in the world. Set to re-mixed and enhanced snippets of one hundred thirty Beatles recordings and out-takes, the acrobatic and dance spectacle is a journey through World War II, the 1960s era of Beatlemania, and the Beatles' last years together making studio albums. The show is filled with characters from Beatles songs, including Mr. Kite, Lady Madonna, the walrus, and Sgt. Pepper, and is a psychedelic parade of tunes such as "Lucy in the Sky with Diamonds" and "A Day in the Life." For the first time ever in a Cirque show, the music was the lead, and the performers were the supporting cast. The music was enhanced by the beat, not merely adorned by it.

One of the first moves Laliberté had made was to bring in Beatles producer Sir George Martin and his son Giles to dig up old master recordings from the band's vaults. They then spent years in studio reworking the songs digitally. "We wanted it to be a performance again for the Beatles," Giles Martin told *MacLean's* magazine. "The idea was to try and make people listen again, as opposed to taking the songs for granted."

This was a true rock and roll experience that audiences would line up to see at the $130-million theatre, furnished with 6,341 speakers and 2,013 theatre-in-the-round seats. French designer Jean Rabasse custom-designed each seat with three speakers, including a pair in the headrest. The stage was Cirque's most elaborate to date, sporting nine lifts and eight automated tracks and trolleys.

It was thought the real challenge might be getting Beatles fans to embrace the concept of *Love*. But no one in the world could have done this task better than Laliberté's ambitious team at Cirque du Soleil.

"I tried to get inspired by the lyrics, but also by the moments and the motions of their careers," the show's concept creator, Dominic Champagne, says. "We tried to be spiritual and physical without trying to be too didactic. I didn't want to do the live version of the *Beatles Anthology*. We're not here to teach the Beatles story to people."

Laliberté projected that the show would be sold out for the next ten years at least. "The way the show is going now, it could be sold out for the next hundred years," says Dawn Olsen, editor of the online celebrity site Glosslip.com. "I saw the show with my husband, and we were completely taken in and moved. We had tears rolling down our cheeks. It was such a beautiful and amazing experience. It was truly an experience."

At the gala premiere on June 30, 2006, the impossible happened. All the surviving members of the Beatles family got together in the same room. Paul McCartney, Ringo Starr and his wife Barbara Bach, Yoko Ono, Olivia Harrison and her son Dhani, Sir George Martin, and even John Lennon's first wife Cynthia and son Julian Lennon all made their way down the red carpet and into the spectacular Mirage theatre. The only one not present was Sean Lennon.

The opening bash was packaged with a high-gloss veneer, a deviation from Cirque's trademark avant-garde openings. But no one seemed to mind; the star-studded opening attracted the likes of Brian Wilson of the Beach Boys, Sheila E, Richard Marx, Paul Reiser, Debbie Harry, Hamish Stuart, and Robert Goulet.

After the spectacular opening, Ringo Starr was quoted as saying: "The music was incredible! I was surprised with the emotion I felt when I heard the voices of George and John. Two of our brothers were in the room, even though they weren't sitting next to us."

Well-respected Fox journalist Roger Friedman was on hand to conduct interviews with the Beatles and members of Cirque du Soleil. In his July 3 report on Fox news, Friedman said that he overheard Paul McCartney boasting with joy to fellow Beatle Ringo Starr, "We were a pretty great group, weren't we?" Cynthia Lennon got emotional when she was interviewed. "I was close to tears at the end. I mean, the show really moved me." At the end of the premiere, McCartney took the stage and received a thunderous ovation when he shouted to the crowd, "To John and George!"

Once again, Laliberté had silenced his critics. He explained to CBSNews.com, "We're not afraid of risking what was our success yesterday in order to explore some new field. We're adventurous. We like the challenge of unknown territory, unknown artistic fields, and that's what stimulates us."

The gala opening of Love was a dual celebration for Laliberté. He had flown in seventy-five family members to celebrate the fiftieth anniversary of his parents, Blandine and Gaston Laliberté. They renewed their vows at a Bellagio hotel wedding chapel before heading to the hotel's high-end eatery, Chef Julian Serrano's Picasso restaurant. "I am what I am from them," Laliberté said. "This is my gift to them."

How could Laliberté ever top the success of *Love* and a Beatles reunion? "We have our work cut out for us for the next six or seven years," he said. "We are, essentially, messengers of good news and carriers of hope. Cirque's objective will remain the same: to contaminate the planet with good creative projects that suggest reasons to hope."

Laliberté wouldn't be slowing down any time soon. He would continue to create new Cirque shows, and he would also create a new career for himself in one of his favourite sidelines—gambling.

# 18

After the *Love* success, Laliberté felt he could go on winning forever. There was no better place to try his acumen than in the cardrooms of Las Vegas. At this point he'd been living there for many years, and in a society that permits gambling to flourish, he had inevitably spent many all-nighters playing backgammon and blackjack at casinos on the Strip.

He could afford to gamble worry-free. By 2007, Laliberté had received numerous awards and accolades from around the world, including The Order of Canada and designation as one of *Time* magazine's one hundred most influential people in the world. He had been named the 664th richest man in the world by *Forbes* magazine, with a fortune valued at $1.5 billion. The math and social skills of poker appealed to Laliberté. He started getting in on games at Bobby's Room at the Bellagio hotel, home of the Cirque du Soleil show *O*. He wanted to have fun, but he also wanted to win.

"I started playing poker for the pleasure and fun of it," Laliberté said. "I learned by reading about it and talking to people. It's a complete game of being intelligent, but also of having your share of luck. It's a very competitive game, and I like competition."

He was familiar with another well known Quebecer who wagers millions in Vegas—René Angélil. In fact, the two had crossed paths several times there. Angélil gave Laliberté some cardroom tips and admitted that he was a compulsive gambler. He talked of losing millions over the years at games where the odds were stacked in favour of the house, as in blackjack and roulette. The futility of that kind of playing had long ago made Angélil vow to play only poker, where the odds were much better.

"René was infatuated by Guy's incredible success," says a mutual musician friend. "It's not as if they'd hang out every night together, though. They had little in common. René certainly did give Guy a mini crash course on poker. Guy was more than willing to listen; not only to René but anyone to else that would give him tips on his new found passion."

Laliberté took up poker in late 2005 and learned the ropes in only a few months as he bought in to the nightly Big Games at Bobby's Room. He quickly demonstrated he was ready to play against the world's best players. His biggest success came at the World Poker Tour championship games in April 2007, in which he won almost $700,000. His success there earned him an invitation to the fourth season of the popular TV show *High Stakes Poker,* which aired in November 2007. All of a sudden, Laliberté as an individual was famous for something totally autonomous from Cirque du Soleil; he had become a star in his own right.

"Guy started getting fan mail from people all over the world because they saw him on TV playing poker," a former Cirque executive says. "With Cirque, the public wouldn't usually know who he was. He'd often stand in the crowd the night of a premiere, listening to its reaction and taking notes. Rarely would someone recognize him. When he started playing poker on TV, he had people recognizing him almost everywhere he went. He had become a full-fledged celebrity. People would stop him and ask for autographs. Leave it to Guy; he's the man with nine lives. He never ceases to stop moving in all kinds of directions. With Guy, you never know what to expect next."

As in his early days of the circus, however, Laliberté had some dues to pay on the poker circuit. Some of the card sharks he competed against had been in the poker business for thirty years. The first year Laliberté competed in big name tournaments, they made mincemeat out of him. As a regular fixture in the online poker scene, Laliberté became the 2007 biggest overall cash game loser at Full Tilt, an Internet poker game site. He lost close to an estimated $7 million playing behind the screen name "Noataima." Laliberté has been suspected of playing behind several other screen names, including "Patatino" and "Elmariachimacho". His competitors would salivate whenever one of those names entered a game, knowing their chances would be good to clean out a rich man's deep pockets.

No matter how costly, losing never deterred Laliberté. The more he lost, the harder he played. In late 2007, he squared off with renowned poker player Doyle Brunson for $818,100, the biggest pot ever on the TV program *High Stakes Poker*; it was one of the highest rated episodes on the American GSN cable network. The legendary Texan, nicknamed Ted Dolly, made a mockery of Laliberté as he raised him to $310,000 and then pushed the remainder of his chips into the pot. When Laliberté raised Ted Dolly, the entire room went silent. Every person looked at him as if he were out of his mind. The four other players had already bowed out, leaving just Brunson and Laliberté, whom Brunson called "the billionaire amateur." Needless to say, Brunson walked off with the entire pot. After the record hand, Brunson said of Laliberté, "When you don't make a pair for eight hours, you go crazy."

Laliberté made it clear to his fellow competitors that he would lose no sleep, no matter how much cash he lost. He told them he could afford to lose the money. He proved his point to the world in December 2007, when he eclipsed his previous record with Brunson with a $1.2 million pot against David Benyamine. When Laliberté realized he had the upper hand, he pleaded with Benyamine to back out. "It's a lot of money for you; not for me," he told Benyamine. "I can afford to lose this. You can't." Brunson, who had also been playing, put it in proper perspective as he told Benyamine to think twice. "One day in his life represents your whole life," Brunson told him. Finally, Benyamine took a bailout offer from Laliberté and lost only the original $47,000 he had wagered.

"Guy didn't show up with the intention of cleaning us all out," Brunson later said. "Sure he likes to win, but he's a sincere gentleman. What he did with David was one of the classiest things. He could have taken all David's money, because he knew he had the advantage. But he didn't. He gave him an escape instead of sinking him."

Laliberté's likeable demeanour made him a well-known name on the popular televised poker tournament. He was a hit with the viewers, even if he didn't show the seasoned skill his fellow players exhibited.

"When I first saw him, I knew right away that he was different—a sort of novelty player," says Richard Dewitt, a long-time Vegas poker player and fan of the hit TV show. "His playing was terrible, but he was so likeable that one had to root for him no matter what. There was never a player on the show I found to be more entertaining. He didn't mind losing crazy amounts of money. He'd joke about it to other players, telling them he could afford to lose all that money because he was a billionaire. The fact that he dressed so casual, often in a T-shirt and baseball cap, was even more alluring. It's not every day you see a person who's worth that much act so casual."

Due to Laliberté's heavy Cirque schedule the following year, he was forced to cut down his appearances on the poker circuit. When he returned in April 2008, his fellow players on the circuit couldn't have been happier. They anticipated he'd wager high stakes again no matter how bad a hand he was dealt.

"His first match back, he lost over $200,000," Dewitt says. "The other players joked how good it was to have him back. Guy appeared thrilled, no matter how much he was down. What an expensive way to spend an evening! But as he often said on the show, no matter how much he loses, he never feels its impact."

Laliberté promised anyone who would listen that he would keep improving. His card playing reminded many of how he ran Cirque du Soleil back in its early days, such as when he took the huge gamble of bringing Cirque to L.A. on one-way tickets. He has often said that in poker he relies on the same street-smarts that he learned early in his career.

"You can get killed pretty fast," Laliberté said in November 2008. "In the street you have to develop that instinct of trusting people and reading people, because that instinct is your life saver. That's something you can definitely apply in the game . . . In some ways, we're still a bunch of little street kids."

19 As the world eagerly watches to see what will happen next with Cirque du Soleil, Laliberté readily acknowledges that all eyes are glued to him. By no means have Laliberté and Cirque du Soleil avoided bumps and potholes. But if rough roads put him in a state of agitation, his experience has nevertheless taught him to avoid one thing above all—panic.

"Business is difficult," Laliberté said in a PBS TV interview. "But it can be approached in two ways: seriously, or the same way you're doing your job, with an entertainment aspect, with pleasure, with fun. And we decided to try to make it fun."

Nevertheless, he's often been accused over the years of exploiting some of his performers, especially those from parts of Russia and the Far East.

"I gave up my whole life to be in Cirque du Soleil and ended up ruining my life," a Russian acrobat says. "I was not well paid, I got injured, and now I have nothing left. They use you when you're in good shape, but when things get tough they will replace you in a second. That's how it works, unfortunately. Some performers get paid well if they have skills that are very rare. But for performers like myself, we're low paid, work ridiculously long hours, and have very short careers. It's not the amazing opportunity most people think it is."

Discontent amongst performers has sometimes led to revolts against the company's upper hierarchy. For instance, during a northern-California run of the highly acclaimed production *Kooza* in February 2008, numerous performers and musicians quit over a dispute with Cirque du Soleil management about pay and work conditions. *Kooza* was a show in which the traditional circus acts of acrobatics and clowning were combined. Performers like Jason Berrent, Theresa Bailey, Chris Bailey, Elodi Dufuo, and Alex Shirin led the employee revolt over working conditions. They tried to round up as many performers as they could for a walkout. Even though they had all signed Cirque's customary airtight performer contracts, it was not enough to stop them from walking out, ready to sacrifice themselves to any legal consequences Cirque might in turn levy against them.

"Cirque du Soleil can be a very aggressive operation," one of the performers says. "They don't let anything stand in their way. Guy Laliberté has never been accused of overpaying anyone except himself, which is perfectly fine with me. But he's got to impose better conditions for his performers or he'll have a lot of unhappy people on his hands. What happened on the *Kooza* tour was not fair to the well-being of the performers. The conditions were impossible and inhuman. That's why we walked out. We had had enough of being treated without respect and like we didn't have rights."

One person close to the performers commented online about what went down on the *Kooza* tour. He said that almost the entire cast had considered quitting. "As a person close to the performers who are walking out, I can assure you that they are all leaving because they are all unhappy," he said. "The original cast of *Kooza* consists of many artists and musicians who are extremely talented, who know their worth, and who are used to a certain type of treatment. But apparently the ones in management positions at *Kooza* are not all experienced and do not always treat the artists with respect."

Laliberté does not deny that there have been rumblings by performers in his company over the years. He makes it clear, however, that having been a performer himself until 1987, he is able to sympathize about the gruelling effects that working for Cirque might have. But, he says convincingly, those who work for his company are provided valuable benefits and opportunities that cannot be found with any other circus company in the world.

"You can't do it unless you have passion and pleasure in doing it," he told *Maclean's* magazine. "I think you have to be a little mad to be a circus performer. It's a wild job . . . You have the Russians who are doing triples in the air—guys who run the most risk of breaking their neck—and five minutes before they go on they're smoking a cigarette, and they'll drink half a bottle of vodka the day after . . .There are fights and depressions. One day, we had a clown arrive with such a big depression. Imagine, the guy is supposed to make people laugh, and he's crying for twenty hours. What do you do?"

Many performers who have worked for Cirque over the years stand by Laliberté. "If you join Cirque and get jealous of how much money Guy makes, then you should quit immediately," says "Alex," a former Cirque clown. "Guy runs a business and took many risks throughout the years. Like any other business owner, he's entitled to make as much money as possible. Sure, he demands hard work from his performers, but it's in their best interest. You can't perform at such a high level without putting in the required work. It's impossible. The performers who complain should wake up and smell the coffee. Without Guy Laliberté, they would be doing some boring office job. He's created so much opportunity, not only for Quebec performers but for performers everywhere in the world."

Laliberté has faced his share of lawsuits from employees in his company and has relied on his team of high-priced lawyers to do some significant damage control. His most common response to lawsuits has been to drag his opponents through the courts until media pressures lead him to settle to avoid further damage to Cirque's reputation. It is the strategy he used to deal with what was perhaps the highest profile complaint against his organization.

Gymnast Matthew Cusick had begun training for Cirque's *Mystère* in 2002 before he informed two Cirque doctors that he was HIV positive. He had been living with HIV for ten years. After intensive physical examinations, both doctors cleared Cusick to perform; yet in April 2003, Cusick was informed by Cirque officials that he was being fired. They called him "a known safety hazard" who posed a threat to other Cirque performers, its crew, and even its audiences. After an hour-long discussion, Cirque officials told Cusick he had to leave the premises and forced him to hand over his ID badge.

Cusick enlisted the services of Lambda Legal, North America's oldest and largest organization representing the legal rights of gay people and people with HIV/AIDS. Cusick claimed that his firing was highly discriminatory and violated the 1990 Americans with Disabilities Act, which prohibits discrimination on the basis of disability. Laliberté and his team of lawyers decided to fight Cusick's action vigorously in the courts, until the media started getting involved.

"He tried to discredit Cusick by having the Cirque publicists issue a press release saying how dangerous Cusick's HIV could be to the other performers. People saw through this attempt to ruin Cusick's credibility. It completely backfired, and the reputation of the circus was at stake. Guy had to settle and apologize to Cusick before it got further out of hand."

On April 22, 2004, Cirque du Soleil finally agreed to an out-of-court settlement with Cusick and paid him $600,000. To this day, Cirque's position is that it was strictly a safety issue rather than an act of discrimination. As part of the settlement, Cirque agreed to review its attitude toward HIV-positive applicants and to subject its employees to an anti-discrimination training program.

"The heat was on Cirque du Soleil because of Cusick's case," the former executive says. "Guy Laliberté wasn't against HIV-positive people; in fact, over the years Cirque has employed many people who had AIDS. What happened here was that Cirque made a grave error in firing Cusick without proper justification. Initially, Guy had no choice but to stand by his people and fight Cusick. Guy does not take it lightly when people try to sue him. You can't blame him; he needs to protect the empire he has worked so hard to create. I think Guy knew deep down that Cirque was wrong in that particular case, and that's why he ended up settling. Guy has been accused of many things in his life, but if there's one thing I know for sure, it's that over the years he's been extremely sympathetic to people with HIV. Many of his close friends in the '80s and '90s died of AIDS. The last thing he'd ever do intentionally is discriminate against someone carrying the virus."

In December 2007, acrobat Olga Vershinina filed a lawsuit against Cirque over a fall that broke her back and pelvis and shattered the bones in her feet. The fall ultimately ended her career. In her lawsuit she claimed the injuries she suffered occurred because of unsafe practices at Cirque.

Karen Tranor, a nurse, was in the audience of the *Zumanity* performance when Vershinina and a male acrobat fell almost thirty-five feet during their act. Tranor later spoke of the inept medical care at the site of the accident.

"The biggest problem I had was with the response time and actual techniques," Tranor said. "When they placed the man on the spinal board they did the proper thing; they rolled him. With the female, they lifted!"

Immediately, Cirque officials went on the defensive and spoke out about how safe the conditions at Cirque have been over the years.

"The company has an unprecedented track record of safety," said Anita Nelving, a PR spokesperson for Cirque. "It's unfortunate that this happened, of course. We know there is risk with any type of circus act performed, but it's our role as a circus company to minimize risks, and we take that very seriously."

Laliberté has repeatedly stressed that Cirque has a full medical staff on hand in case of injury or accident. But he stresses that accidents will happen, regardless of how many safety measures Cirque imposes.

"Anyone who thinks there's no health and personal risk involved in joining Cirque should not apply," says journalist Esmond Choueke. "It would be foolish to think there would be no incidents in something as intense and dangerous as performing as an acrobat or stuntman. It would be the same thing as an NHL hockey player trying to sue his team because he got injured. They know what they're getting into when they sign up, and in the contracts they sign, they waive their right to sue. Anyone who blames Guy or Cirque for an injury is wrong. Things happen that can't be prevented. That's why Cirque pays millions each year to its insurance company to settle such incidents."

Despite the numerous criticisms about his lack of generosity regarding the working conditions for Cirque performers, Laliberté obsessively helps less fortunate people around the world. His frequent meetings and conversations with U2 singer Bono helped inspire him to take affirmative action. As perhaps the world's richest ex-homeless person, which might be said of his busking days in Europe, Laliberté and Cirque have donated millions to homeless organizations around the world. Like Bono, one of his chief missions has been to help eradicate poverty.

Laliberté has received numerous awards for his philanthropy, including the 2007 Humanitarian Award for his pledge to eliminate poverty by giving everybody access to water. Laliberté has committed $100 million over the next twenty-five years to his One Drop Foundation to help fund projects to rebuild water wells and provide drinking water in poor countries. He announced his pledge on October 29, 2007, in front of a packed audience that included Prince Albert II of Monaco and Jeremy Hobbs, executive director of Oxfam International. The CEO of the Royal Bank of Canada Financial Group was in attendance and announced his company would contribute $10 million to the new foundation.

At the foundation's website, onedrop.org, Laliberté explains his ambitious program. "Every eight seconds, a child dies for lack of drinking water," he writes. "Isn't that sufficient reason to take action? For years, I roamed the planet as a street performer. Earning a living in the streets put me in touch with the poverty and distress of thousands of men, women, and children. A little naïvely, no doubt, I told myself that the world would be a better place if its six billion inhabitants would all put on clown noses . . . In time, that dream became Cirque du Soleil."

When I was friends with Laliberté's ex-lover Rizia Moreira, she told me that she had seen Laliberté's will. She said Laliberté was adamant on making sure his fortune would be distributed to good causes, leaving one third to his children, another third to the development of Cirque du Soleil, and one third to a charity of his choice.

"Guy wants to continue helping people long after he passes on," she said. "When I was with him I saw his will. No matter how much I've fallen out with him over the years, I must say how much I respect him for wanting to help poor people around the world. He has a conscience; maybe not for me, but definitely for poor people."

# EPILOGUE

By the end of 2008, it seemed that Cirque du Soleil might have its first ever flop on its hands. Magician Criss Angel's Las Vegas show, *Believe*, had been savaged by critics and the public. According to Vegasnews.com, fans flew in from as far away as London to see the show and came away worse than unimpressed. The article quotes the *Las Vegas Review Journal*'s review of the show, which rated it a "waste of time" and a "dead end" that "literally bored audience members to sleep."

The popular blogger Perez Hilton attended the show and sent real-time text message reports to his fans as it progressed, stating that *Believe* was "unbelievably bad" and that he would rather be getting a root canal. At the end of the show, Angel, who had evidently heard from his people about Hilton's tweets, asked Hilton to stand up and then hurled insults at him from the stage, calling him an asshole and a douchebag. This prompted Cirque to issue a public apology to Hilton for Angel's inappropriate behaviour.

Most critics believe it's only a matter of time until the show is cancelled. One wonders if Laliberté will, once again, emerge from crisis stronger than ever.

Even if Cirque is taking a hit with *Believe*, in early 2009, Laliberté is probably in the best shape of his life, both personally and financially. Cirque has scheduled nineteen touring shows throughout the world and despite the cold of a global economic recession is planning to expand more than ever.

He is skirting the worst economic downturn since the Great Depression by applying his long-learned skills: an unconventional business style and shrewd positioning. Back in 2001, he bought out his lifelong friend and partner Daniel Gauthier for a reported $800 million. Gauthier had helped Cirque develop into one of the world's leading showbiz empires alongside others like Disney and the U.K.-based Merlin Entertainments, which runs Madame Tussaud's and the London Eye. When Gauthier decided it was time to move on, his departure left Laliberté with ninety-eight percent ownership of Cirque du Soleil.

For years Laliberté remained reluctant to sell shares in Cirque, despite numerous offers from private equity investors. Finally, in August 2008, Laliberté decided to pursue additional funding that would allow him to expand the circus more aggressively. At the time, Cirque du Soleil was doing annual sales of close to a billion dollars, attracting ten million spectators a year on five continents. It had six permanent venues in Las Vegas, plus one in Orlando, Florida, and another in the planning for the Kodak theatre in Los Angeles. Another permanent show is set to open in the emerging world business centre of Dubai, in the United Arab Emirates.

Laliberté sold a twenty percent stake in Cirque du Soleil to two units of Dubai World, a holding company, for an estimated $400 million. Dubai World's property developer Nakheel and investment company Istithmar World Capital agreed to build a theatre with Cirque on the extraordinary palm-shaped islands Nakheel developed off Dubai's coast. The 1,800-seat state-of-the-art facility is expected to open in the summer of 2011. The agreement still keeps Laliberté in firm control of Cirque.

"This partnership is the best of both worlds for me and my management team," Laliberté says. "We can keep control of our creative challenges and operations while accelerating our growth, doing projects all over the world."

This seed had been planted when Laliberté learned Dubai was planning to inject more than $350 billion into entertainment projects over the next twelve years. He had flown there many times on his luxurious private Global Express jet, on which he apparently has had painted a signature image of a giant ice cream sundae dripping with hot fudge sauce. The circus ringmaster flying to Dubai in a hot fudge sundae is fitting, as Cirque's 2007 show *Quidam* was the most successful single entertainment event ever to be staged in Dubai, with more than one hundred thousand people buying tickets to the month-long engagement. Success drips off Laliberté.

"Guy's not the man to write ten-page analytical memos," Jacques Renaud, a longtime Cirque executive, told journalist Benoît Aubin. "His diagnoses are spontaneous, instinctive, intuitive, and visionary. He's always on the money."

For many years there has been a long list of investors wanting to buy the company outright from Laliberté, according to Cirque du Soleil company president and CEO, Daniel Lamarre. "Many of them were quite agressive," Lamarre told Tony Wong of the *Toronto Star*. "But others knew that Guy would never sell. He always refused in the past."

Until the Dubai offer came along, Lamarre admitted, it seemed likely that Laliberté would hold his full stake in the company for many more years. "Nakheel was really intriguing to us," Lamarre said. "The more we started to talk, the more we realized this had great potential for everyone . . . We haven't seen too many organizations do a deal with a giant like Dubai and, at the end of the day, keep eighty percent of the company. So we are still Canadian."

While 2009 rolls on and the world economy tanks, Laliberté's solidly Canadian company is in a position to move forward with plans to celebrate Cirque du Soleil's twenty-fifth anniversary. *Cirque 2009* —a new touring show that premiered in Montreal's Old Port in April —marks the celebration, and also marks the twenty-fifth show created and produced by Cirque since it began on June 16, 1984. Laliberté has promised that the show is vastly different from anything Cirque has produced in the past, with insects and their place in the ecosystem as the main theme.

"It has been twenty-five years of dreams, and the dreams will continue," Laliberté told a packed news conference at Cirque's head offices in Montreal, at the launch of the twenty-fifth anniversary media blitz. Laliberté said emphatically that Cirque is watching every dollar it spends more closely than ever, but that plans to expand would not be slowed down. He added that he had tightened his belt around the anniversary festivities and that they would be "modest" compared to past Cirque celebrations.

He announced that the anniversary would include the launching of two new circuses in Montreal and Vegas, a new book on Cirque costumes, the best of Cirque music on a commemorative CD, as well as a spectacular forty-five-minute fireworks tribute to Cirque on closing night of the 2009 international fireworks festival in Montreal.

Laliberté also announced that a new show paying tribute to Elvis would open December 16, 2009, at the Aria Resort & Casino at MGM Mirage's $8.8-billion CityCenter development in Las Vegas.

"We have accomplished our financial goals of the last year, and so far the first month of the year is exactly on target," Laliberté said. "And we hope we will be strong enough to go through the crisis. But are we bulletproof to a great depression? Probably not."

His Christmas present for the artists of the Cirque show Zaia was a handbag made from the tarp of an old Cirque *grand chapiteau*, or big top. The recycled material bags were a fit for Cirque's eco-friendly vision and a great gift of understated class during an economic recession.

"No matter what happens, Guy constantly stays on top of things," a former Cirque executive says. "During the recession, what does he give out to his performers for Christmas? A stunning handbag recycled from an old Cirque tent. It was in the Cirque's traditional yellow and blue colors. What a creative and cost-efficient way to give something unique to his workers. The man's a total genius."

While many entrepreneurs are seeing their net worth plummet like never before, according to *Forbes*, Laliberté's net worth has soared forty-seven percent to $2.5 billion. Of the 1,125 billionaires who made the *Forbes* list in 2008, 373 fell off the next year—the highest drop since 2003. Positioned at number 707 on the list in 2008, Laliberté was one of only 44 billionaires who added to their fortunes in the following twelve months, bringing him up 446 places to position 261 in 2009. He is not always great at poker, but he certainly showed foresight when he gambled and sold twenty percent of his shares in Cirque just a few months before Wall Street crashed.

"A lot of people who are on the list this year sold portions of their business at the height of the economy, a little over a year ago," CEO Steve Forbes said. "Yes, you need luck, but don't always think you can create your luck. That is called hubris."

In Canada, only twenty of the twenty-five billionaires listed in 2008 remained. The publishing-baron Thomson family ranked first at

$13 billion, down from the previous year's $18.9 billion. Montreal's eighty-two-year-old head of Power Corp, Paul Desmarais, ranked fifth on the list after his fortune plunged to $2.6 billion, while Laliberté bypassed him and jumped to fourth place. In Quebec, Laliberté was by far the youngest of the province's six billionaires.

"Gambling has always been in my blood, but never to the point of putting the things I've built in danger," Laliberté has said. Clearly, Cirque is one of a small number of companies that can weather the world economic storm without many scratches.

Unlike almost every other large company that is laying off alarming rates of employees, Cirque du Soleil is intent on protecting its 4,200 employees worldwide.

"We are not dupes, naïve, or innocents," Daniel Lamarre said. "Protecting the livelihood of the thousands of families that contribute ceaselessly to our success is one of our surest values."

Laliberté's decisions are magical, shrewd, and nothing less than anyone expected of him. In April 2009, he told *The New York Times* that although attendance at his six full-time Vegas shows was down seven percent, Cirque's touring shows were up seven per cent. "We've gone through three recessions in Cirque history," Laliberté told *The New York Times*. "And they were all growth periods for us . . . But we are not tsunami-proof. It is a scary crisis in Vegas—our partners have so much debt."

Laliberté is fighting the recession head-on. In several of the locations where Cirque is performing and where the downturn has hit hardest, Laliberté has lowered ticket prices twenty percent, giving a break to those who couldn't normally afford to see a Cirque show. In early March 2009, Cirque offered Florida residents a discount for its category two seats at its La Nouba show—$64 per person instead of $84.

"The reason why Guy is so successful is because he always stays on top of things and never gets too complacent," a former Cirque executive says. "He's a perfectionist who likes to be well informed. His most amazing characteristic is being able to turn things around, no matter what situation he puts himself into. Very few people today are able to do that."

Laliberté is not mysterious about his own future. He has often said that someday he wants to travel into space, and he also is keen on expanding his charitable contributions to the world. After twenty-five years of running Cirque, his dream has not wavered much from the days he started out in Baie-Saint-Paul with his gang of street performing friends.

As the world continues to hail Laliberté's genius and Cirque's widespred appeal, Laliberté continues to branch out and invest in other exploits such as nightclubs, restaurants, and his One Drop Foundation.

He will be remembered as one of the biggest innovators and re-creators ever of the circus. "We didn't reinvent the circus," Laliberté says. "We repackaged it in a much more modern way . . . Circus arts have so much historical background that I don't think it is a mature industry. I think that it needs some dusting off every twenty years or so."

Laliberté shows he is a consummate dreamer by insisting that even today's Cirque du Soleil is only the tip of the iceberg. Incredibly, there are still barrages of hidden memories in him that eventually will find their way out as brilliant creative ideas.

As a tribute to his millions of fans around the world, everyone attending a Cirque du Soleil show anywhere in the world on June 16, 2009, the date of the twenty-fifth anniversary of the circus, was handed a clown nose to be worn during the show. When he started Cirque, he wished for everyone in the world to lighten up and not take themselves too seriously. He insists that everyone in the world should wear a red clown nose, at least for a second.

"I knew I could live my dream of travelling, entertaining, and having fun," Guy Laliberté told *The Hollywood Reporter*. "I am blessed for what I have, but I believed in it from the beginning. Today, the dream is the same: I still want to travel, I still want to entertain, and I most certainly still want to have fun."

*  *  *

# POST SCRIPTUM

A couple of days before Transit went to press for the first edition of this book, a high profile ex-hooker contacted me with incredible details of her times with Laliberté. Natalie McLennan, originally from Montreal, graced the July 2005 cover of *New York* magazine for its story on her, "N.Y.'s #1 Escort Reveals All."

McLennan, a stunning brunette who looks more like a supermodel than a call girl, was widely acknowledged as being Manhattan's highest-paid escort, at $2,000 an hour. She dated her notorious pimp boss, Jason Itzler, and was hired by numerous A-list actors, NFL quarterbacks, and well-known politicians to perform in the bedroom. In 2008, McLennan received worldwide attention, including an interview on Larry King Live, when it was revealed by the media that she was the person who had trained disgraced New York Governor Eliot Spitzer's long-time hooker, Ashley Dupré.

McLennan was credited with grooming the nineteen-year-old Dupré, showing her the tricks of the escort trade for Manhattan's top escort agency, NY Confidential.

McLennan sent me an email on May 28, 2009 saying, "Shit Ian, you should have interviewed me for the Guy Laliberté book, I have some great stories . . . NYC circa 2002-2005. XO, Natalie." I wrote McLennan back asking her to write an account of her time with Laliberté. She agreed to do it. When I received her story a few days later, it was most revealing. McLennan, who penned a book about her experiences as an escort called *The Price*, did not spare any details.

### Intimate Encounters with Guy Laliberté

Before I became an escort, but after I'd become a regular on the New York party scene, New York City was in a post-9/11 shambles, and the party people (myself included) were partying harder than ever. There's nothing like celebrating the end of the world. I was living with a New York legend—just friends of course. We'll call him *A*, for short. His loft was at 111 Reade Street, between Church and Broadway. It had high ceilings, gorgeous furniture from Thailand and the Middle East, and a revolving door of models, photographers, drug dealers, and other nightlife types. I had been trying for months to find my way into the movie industry but had instead ended up in more than a couple of producers' beds. Now I was finding I was going to fewer and fewer auditions and to more and more parties.

Then, on one of the first warm, almost springlike nights of the season, I met Guy Laliberté. He was already a legend in my eyes. Growing up in Montreal, I had heard endless stories about him.

His parties every year during the Montreal Grand Prix were famous for their giant bowls of ecstasy and celebrities from all over the world, especially the Hollywood variety.

It happened, of course, at a party. A hosted some of the best after-hours parties at his loft, and after a few weeks living with him, I had met everyone. On this Friday night, the loft was already buzzing with activity, and it was barely even dark out yet. A came in to wake me up from a disco nap I had been taking in his bed. "Sweetheart, we've got to get you dressed. We're going out tonight." I didn't budge. "Where?" I asked. I hadn't slept in weeks and was going to need some serious inspiration to get up to go anywhere. A delivered it. "Guy's in town. We have to take care of him." That's sort of the way the New York party circuit works. The native New Yorkers and transplants hold down the scene 365 days a year, keeping the clubs busy and the vibe cool. And almost every night someone new is in town—an actor, rock star, royalty—someone who needs to be shown a good time. A was from L.A. with big friends with huge money and one thing in common—they loved to party. Everything from coke to ecstasy, GHB, and Special K to the extreme party drug, freebase.

At the mention of Guy's name, my eyes popped open, and I was fully awake. Finally, I knew I was really in the right circle; I'd been adopted by the elite. A was already standing in front of the walk-in closet looking through the racks of dresses and designer clothes, all left behind by his ex-girlfriend. A beautiful, blond Versace model, she'd been overwhelmed by the scene and the drugs, as well as an eating disorder it was rumoured, and had been sent home. Coincidentally, she was also from Montreal.

The clothes were fantastic, but unfortunately, in my party-girl state, almost everything was too big. I was maybe ninety pounds and five-foot-four. Everything was sample size, but my being model size zero meant that everything was too big and too long on me. Finally, we found a drapey black top that was barely long enough to pass as a dress but would probably do fine. I went to the bathroom, took a quick shower, shaved my legs, and started putting on some makeup. *A* peeked his head in the bathroom, "Shit, we should have gone tanning." I was so pale, and his Middle Eastern skin was almost as light as mine. "I have bronzer," I offered. He laughed and told me to hurry up. We had to meet everyone at Indochine on Lafayette in twenty minutes for dinner. I suddenly remembered I was supposed to work at Noel Ashman's club, Veruka, that night. I'd lost every other job due to my after-hours lifestyle and needed the one night a week the manager, Tim, gave me out of pity. I told *A* the problem. He said cancel. I wavered for a second. Weekly income to eat and party or hanging out with Guy Laliberté? I picked up the cordless house phone and dialled Tim's number, leaving him a message that I couldn't work, that I was sick as usual.

We arrived late to Indochine, really late. We had gotten stuck on Reade Street waiting for our dealer to arrive, and then, before we left, had cooked up some freebase and done a few hits. I took small ones. I didn't want to be too spaced out and unable to hold a conversation. A gave me a bag of powder to keep in my purse for the night.

At Indochine, there was a big table of people. I knew a couple of them, guys who were *A*'s friends and regulars at all the weekly parties, but there were a lot of girls I didn't recognize, not the usual crowd. They were obviously done eating (or maybe they never bothered). A few bottles of Veuve stood on the table, along with some bottles of Grey Goose and mixers. *A* poured us some drinks, and I drank mine. He finished his and poured us each another one. Then

Guy arrived. He was with one other person, a guy I sort of knew. The night was getting started. When I was introduced to Guy, he kissed me on both cheeks, Montreal-style. I stayed close to him, and we talked a little. He was smiling and in a great mood.

Afterwards, we moved across the street to Pangaea, Michael Ault's club. It had been open a little less than a year, and it was really the busiest and most fun place to be most nights. I had interviewed to be a cocktail waitress there before they opened but had opted at the time to work at another place, Stephen Baldwin's club, Luahn, instead. Michael Ault himself seated us at the back under the DJ booth along the right wall. Bottles appeared at the table, and I jumped up on the banquette and started dancing. I didn't move from there all night. I didn't even have to bother going to the bathroom to do my bumps of coke; the guys were spilling out hills onto backs of their hands and sticking it under everyone's noses.

We were in our own little bubble, and sometime around 2 AM I learned we were going to relocate. *A* took me aside and said, "I'm going home. Stay with Guy; he wants you to stay." He gave me a wink and in front of me, took the guy who'd arrived with Guy all those hours earlier at Indochine aside and said, "Make sure you take care of her." The friend pulled me close and kissed the top of my head, then he grabbed my hand and pulled me into the cab with Guy. There was another girl there, too, a blond. Her name was Mischa, and she was Russian. We had been dancing together all night at Pangaea. I asked the cab driver to tune the radio to 103.5, and then I started kissing Mischa. The rest of the cab ride was a blur of bumps of coke and all of us making out. I made sure to only make out with Guy and not his friend. I remembered what *A* had told me. Guy wanted me there.

We arrived at Float, on 52nd Street, and went upstairs to the third floor right away. By the time we left, I'd taken a pill—some kind of ecstasy—and I was wearing someone's Gucci sunglasses. As we were leaving, Guy grabbed my hand, then I grabbed Mischa's hand, and we all went down the stairs together, everyone else following behind.

At this point I was blitzed. I know we walked only a few blocks to Guy's hotel, but I have no idea which hotel it was. Guy had a huge suite with multiple living rooms and a big bedroom with French doors. People started pouring drinks and doing bumps of coke. Guy's friend took me into the bedroom right away and closed the doors. He pulled open a big sandwich baggie of coke, broke off a big rock, and said, "Here, is that enough? Is that enough for what you need?" I looked at the rock and nodded. He gestured to the bathroom, "You can go in there. I'll make sure no one comes in." I went into the bathroom and put the rock down on the vanity. I broke off a little piece, crushed it with my Canadian ID, and snorted it with a little straw I kept in my purse. While I was touching up my makeup, I took the plastic off my pack of cigarettes and dropped the rock in it.

Then I stopped in my tracks. He thought I was going to cook it into freebase and smoke it. Wow, *A*'s and my reputation as party people had really preceded us, as if they thought I needed to smoke. And that didn't really sit with me very well; I was going to have to discuss it with *A*. I didn't want to be known as that sort of a girl. But it was considerate all the same that they had thought to tend to my drug habits.

I came out of the bathroom and found Guy and Mischa on the bed. Guy smiled and pulled me onto the bed with them. This was fun, I thought. Guy wanted me and Mischa to make out some more but she was a little hesitant. Away from Pangaea and the chaos of the cab ride, she had become a little more timid. This wasn't just flirting. Now we were actually in bed; this was going somewhere. Never shy with girls, I didn't mind. I started to go down on her just as the friend came into the room and smiled at Guy. "Tu es content, toi?" he asked in French. Guy just laughed. The friend sat on the bed for a few minutes, but when Guy started making out with me, he discreetly got up and closed the French doors behind him. The blaring noise of the music and party in the rest of the suite suddenly became a only dull roar in the background, and it was just the three of us. We played, we laughed, we took off all our clothes. Guy was like the Cirque du Soleil in bed. That's how I will always remember that night. He was lifting me up off the bed, he was loud, he was fun. Mischa was still a little reluctant. Guy put on a condom and started having sex with her, but she was just doing it; it wasn't really about feeling good. The ecstasy was hitting me really hard, and I just wanted Guy to touch me. It didn't bother me that Mischa was in the bed with us.

After hours of sex, we both eventually fell asleep, and when I woke up, the suite was much quieter. I put my top/dress on, opened the bedroom doors and went into the living room, where I sat down next to my friend Mauro, the manager at ManRay. "I didn't know you were here," he said. He smiled and I giggled, then he handed me a rolled-up bill. I looked at the table in front of me. There was a mountain of coke on it. I was tempted, but now that I was awake again, I really felt like going home to Reade Street. This was next-day after-hours partying, and I didn't know these people that well. I wanted to hang out with *A*.

I went back into the bedroom. Guy was snoring a little (everyone does when they do coke), and I tried to be quiet as I gathered my shoes and purse and put myself together As I was getting ready to leave, I asked Mauro if I could borrow twenty dollars to get home. Leaving the hotel, I still felt a bit disoriented and didn't know where I was exactly. I was definitely not sober. I hailed a cab and made it all the way downtown in just a few minutes. At least it was Saturday, and only a few people had seen me in my barely-a-dress dress.

I buzzed the loft, and *A* came down to open the door. We walked up the stairs, and I could tell he'd been smoking all night. He was lucid and funny and cuddly with me. He asked me if I had had fun as he loaded up a bong for me to take a hit of freebase. I nodded and exhaled a huge hit of smoke. Just then before I would have crashed and forgotten all about it for a few hours, I remembered the boulder of coke in my purse. I pulled it out and smiled as I handed it to *A*. "I guess we aren't sleeping for a while." I laughed. "Did you get his number?" he asked. I was confused and shook my head no. What did he mean? Oh. Did I get Guy's number? Then A shook his head at me and said, "You're unbelievable. I introduce you to a billionaire, and you don't even get his number."

Cut to three years later, early 2005. I am well into my short but wild ride as New York's number-one escort. I was recently estranged from my pimp/boyfriend Jason Itzler and ecstatic to be free at last. Together with my best girlfriend and roommate Jordan, I had decided to celebrate my twenty-fifth birthday cross-country style. The plan was to jet-set around the U.S., doing lots of skiing—code for coke up the nose. We were going to start in New York, our home sweet home, and had booked tickets to Vegas at the insistence of my long-time friend Alex Martini, a New York nightlife legend. We then were going to proceed to L.A. and finally back to New York. The whole celebration was to span a minimum of two months with little time for sleep. This was the time in my life when I had too much money, too much cash really. I spent it like every nouveau riche—fast.

Alex wanted us meet him in Vegas for the opening of Guy's new Cirque show, *Ka*. He said he would have a suite at the MGM waiting for us as well as tickets to the show. What better way to celebrate my birthday than with the best party person in the world—Guy! I had already seen the show with a client in early January during the preview period. That had been my first time in Vegas. We had stayed at the Belagio. The entire thing had been a whirlwind of champagne, caviar, and, of course, a $20,000 paycheque.

I had told Alex that if tickets for the show were tight, I could busy myself with other things. Jordan and I knew we had some serious shopping to do. After all, I hadn't seen Guy in a few years, and I wanted to impress him, I thought it would make him proud to see his fellow Montrealer earning lots of U.S. dollars just like him. It was the wee hours of the morning, so after booking our tickets online we jumped on Adidas.com and ordered matching purple camouflage track suits to wear on the plane.

Alex told me Guy lived in a $30,000-a-month mansion at the MGM. Okay, I wasn't doing that well by comparison, but it's all an illusion, right? Jordan and I packed our best Manolos and were on our way. We had already been to see our dealer down on Delancey Street and had come up with a solution for traveling. This was not for the faint of heart. Neither of us was looking to get arrested at the airport because of an eightball of coke and a few grams of some other drogue, but being sober was not an option. So we split what we had into two little packages and rolled it in a little tissue, slipped it into a condom, knotted it, and, at the last minute, in the cab to the airport, tucked it inside our cootchies. Once we passed through security and boarded the plane—getting checked out by Kevin Bacon along the way (I think he liked our matching track suits and Oliver Peoples shades)—we sneaked into the bathroom, took the little packages out, and tucked them into my carry-on.

When we arrived in Vegas, we jumped into a limo and called Alex to let him know we were minutes away. He met us in the lobby with kisses, and we went right upstairs to our room. He said there was a change of plans. He had booked us a private room, but, not to worry, we could stay in the suite if we really wanted to. What he meant all became clear a few minutes later after I had slipped into a dress and heels and we had gone to the suite. I was greeted there by some serious Euro-sleaze. Three of the guys immediately started putting their hands all over me, before they even knew my name. Alex extracted me from their clutches and took me into the bathroom, where, in his sexy Italian lisp, he apologised, saying,

"I'm so sorry baby, they will not leave." He kissed me on the lips, and we did a bump of coke, then special K, and all was forgiven. Alex was one of the first people I had met in New York all those years ago. He always looked out for me. He invited me to the best parties, told me when I needed some sleep, and had even visited me in the hospital when I was sick. I was so happy to have my own room with Jordan, since I was always the polite Canadian and usually found it hard to be firm and tell yucky guys to leave me alone.

Jordan, however, was a lost cause. Somewhere between JFK and the lights of the Vegas Strip she came down with a cold/flu/burnout sickness and said she needed a nap. So she crashed in the room. Alex and I decided to skip dinner and instead sat in the hot tub in the bathroom of the suite with the door closed. We talked about our original party days—pre-escort, pre-9/11, before things got heavy and real. I told him I was in a little trouble with drugs. I could see rehab in my future and then what? He told me not to worry, and, in our usual style, we both did another bump of something.

So when was I going to see Guy finally? We dressed for the show, and I tried to revive Jordan one more time. She was still sleeping and felt hot and sticky, so I left her a little drogue on the bedside table in case she was dope-sick. At the show, Alex led me over to say hi to Guy. He was all smiles and kisses on both cheeks. We took our seats and Alex quietly asked me, "Do you know so-and-so?" referring to Guy's girlfriend. I shook my head no. I told Alex that I hadn't seen Guy since the night we partied in 2002. "She's a little territorial, but then I guess that's to be expected, right?" he said with a little wink. "I guess they don't have an open relationship, right?" I joked back. The lights dimmed, and the show started. I love the Cirque du Soleil, but *Ka* isn't my favourite show. Very big on hydraulics and massive set pieces but not so focused on the artistry and detail that makes their shows so beautiful. We stayed for the first half and then went back to the suite to relax. This was going to be a long night.

And it was. Guy threw a big party for the cast, crew, and all his friends that ended up feeling more like a high-school dance than what we'd all signed up for. Yes, the music was great. A friend of Guy's, who was the DJ at all his parties, was spinning great music, but I spent most of the night wandering around. I got so bored that I even decided to amuse myself with my own personal fashion show, changing clothes about half a dozen times during the night. Gradually it got late by Vegas and even our own crazy three-day standards. Alex walked over to me and seemed just as frustrated as I was. Where was the vibe of the legendary Grand Prix parties or the knockdown-throwdown debauchery from Pangaea?

"Sorry baby, I don't know what is going on. Guy was supposed to move the party back to his place a while ago. Wait here, I'll be right back." After a few minutes, Alex came back and took my hand. We walked for what seemed like forever. I hated to whine, but I had to say it, "This was supposed to be my Vegas birthday party." I was tripping on the carpet in my high heels, and I knew I was almost in Tara Reid drunk-drugged-falling-over-girl territory. Plus, my best friend had passed out. There also was no VIP to keep us safe and happy. I was suddenly feeling lonely and sad—all that birthday stuff. Finally, we walked through some sort of secret garden. Alex knocked on a door, and we landed in a little piece of heaven: Guy's Mansion.

There were only a few people there, but I instantly felt better. The living room opened up onto a swimming pool. I immediately stripped off my clothes and jumped in, sobering up a little at once. All was not lost. When Guy and his small inner entourage of about four arrived a little while later, I was still lounging by the pool in my G-string with Alex beside me in his Italian boxer-briefs. I caught a dirty look from Guy's girlfriend, girlfriend, and I knew this was not going to be a party that ended in a happy threesome with Guy and some Russian girl.

And it wasn't. I still had fun, though. I put my dress back on after the evil-eye cue from the girlfriend, and everyone gave me a great Happy Birthday champagne toast. I returned to our room and my sweaty best friend in the wee hours of the morning and slept the day away. We looked forward to the trouble we would undoubtedly get into in L.A. and Malibu over the next few days.

And that was the last time I saw Guy. I don't know if he read my July 2005 *New York* magazine cover story, which called me "The $2,000-an-hour woman," or if he heard that I ended up in jail.

Nevertheless, I think that if I had gotten his phone number when I had the chance that night at the hotel, I might have called him to bail me out. And I think he would have.

\* \* \* \*

A few days after this book was published, Laliberté hastily called a press conference to announce that, in September 2009, the month he was to turn fifty years old, he intended to become Canada's first space tourist. At a press conference in Moscow, the billionaire announced he would blast off on board a Russian Soyuz spacecraft. His flight would cost around $35 million. Laliberté called his adventure a "poetic social mission" to help increase public awareness of world water issues in conjunction with his One Drop Foundation. "I've been introduced as many things in the past—fire breather, entrepreneur, performer, partier," Laliberté told a jam-packed press conference. "But today, to be introduced as a private space explorer is an enviable and unbelievable feeling."

According to a journalist who has covered Laliberté's career since its beginning, Laliberté called the press conference because he was furious that I had revealed his space plans in this book. "When he read the book and saw the part about him wanting to go into space he hit the ceiling," said journalist Esmond Choueke, who has covered Cirque du Soleil since the mid-1980s and has interviewed Laliberté one-on-one. "He felt threatened because he did not want to be scooped. So he demanded that his staff arrange a press conference before the book started getting media attention."

Guy Laliberté generally controls his public image ruthlessly, and, in the past, Cirque has been successful in scaring publications into not printing any material deemed negative. But this time has been different. A few days before the publication of this book, Quebec's respected news magazine *L'Actualité* ran an excerpt. Caught off guard, Laliberté's representatives responded with uncharacteristic clumsiness. Cirque's director of public relations, Renée-Claude Menard, told the media that my claims about Laliberté's orgies and drug use were "urban legends." She called the book "sensationalism" and said that there weren't sex and drugs at Laliberté's parties. Incredibly, in the same interview, Menard admitted she had not read one paragraph or word of my biography.

"This is the way Laliberté and Cirque have got away controlling the media for years," journalist Choueke said. "As soon as something negative is about to come out, they have their lawyers threatening to sue. Usually, they've been very successful controlling the media. Your book is the first time someone has been able to escape their legal claws."

I responded quickly. In an interview with *Journal de Montréal* reporter Dany Bouchard, I said that writing a book about Laliberté and not mentioning his propensity for sex and drugs would be the equivalent of writing a book about Bob Marley and not mentioning Marley smoked pot. Most likely, I will end up suing Menard and Cirque for defamation. Menard's erroneous and scurrilous statements were based on no knowledge or foundation of what was actually in the book.

A week later, after the book had been shipped to bookstores across Quebec, Laliberté's lawyers sent my publisher a *mise en demeure* —a formal legal notice—demanding that the book be removed from book store shelves within twenty-four hours. In the lawyer's letter, at no point did Laliberté allege that one fact in my book was inaccurate. The only thing he was concerned about was the details I divulged about his relationship with his ex-common-law wife, Rizia Moreira. Moreira. Naturally, my publisher's lawyers responded saying that Laliberté had no right to infringe on the freedom of the press and that the books would not be removed. This reaction seemed to incense Laliberté and Cirque more than ever. However, the climax was yet to come.

When Page Six of the *New York Post* ran the headline "Cirque du So-leil Creator Called Cheater" on May 28, 2009, Laliberté hit the ceiling. A mutual friend of ours in New York told me that Laliberté was furious that the book was getting international attention. A few days later, Page Six ran another story about how Laliberté was trying to stop my book. In the article, they referred to Laliberté as a "bed-hopping scoundrel." "Guy was raging mad about this," the mutual friend said. "He had hoped that the story would not leave Quebec. Now it was making headlines in one of the biggest publications in the world. He needed to react."

A couple of days later, Cirque and Laliberté sent another *mise en demeure* to Canada's most respected news magazine, *MacLean's*, for running the cover story "Guy Laliberté: The Fabulous Story of the Crea-tor of Cirque du Soleil." *MacLean's* called my book "a stunning exposé of the biggest show on earth and its billionaire founder." According to Choueke, Laliberté was now out for blood. His lawyers sent *MacLean's* a letter making numerous erroneous statements. At one point they claimed that the book never covered any of the Cirque's shows. Nothing could be further from the truth. The book discusses how Laliberté created Cirque shows and what went on behind the scenes. They also called me a "gos-sip writer," conveniently forgetting to take note that I'm a *New York Times* best-selling author with a mantle of awards for my accomplish-ments over the years. "You took on a big fish," Choueke warned me "They won't rest until they destroy you. They'll put out things about you that are false and defamatory. They have enough money to drag you through the courts for years. Unfortunately, that's the reality here."

Perhaps my publisher, Pierre Turgeon, summed it up best. Turgeon, one of only two writers ever twice to win Canada's Governor General's Award for writing, said going against Laliberté and the Cirque du Soleil is tantamount to David facing Goliath. "In all my thirty-five years of be-ing in the publishing business, I've never seen anything like this,"

Turgeon said. "Laliberté has no right to demand that the books be removed from the bookstores. The book is very positive. What he's trying to do is against freedom of the press. It would be a scary precedent if he succeeded."

# Index of Names Cited

# Index of Names Cited

# Index of Names Cited

# Index of Names Cited